RIDING IN MOUNTED GAMES

ALLEN RIDER GUIDES

Riding in Mounted Games

Jeanne O'Malley

J.A. Allen

London

Published in Great Britain by
J.A. ALLEN & Co. Ltd
1 Lower Grosvenor Place
London
SW1W OEL

British Library Cataloguing in Publication Data
A catalogue record for this book is available from the British Library.

ISBN 0-85131-580-1

Line drawings: Maggie Raynor
Text and cover design: Nancy Lawrence

Typeset by Textype Typesetters, Cambridge
Printed by Huntsman Offset, Singapore

Dedicated to Terry Thompson, the master of them all

Contents

Preface

As breeds of horses become more and more versatile it seems to me that the people who ride them become more and more specialised. People 'do' dressage and they do it seriously. Riders 'are in training for eventing'. Western Pleasure horses rarely see the outside of an arena lest they mess up their training. 'Dedicated', 'serious', and 'professional' are the highest compliments one can give. Many books on riding and training are ponderous and turgid tomes demanding more discipline than the sport they describe. Or they are written with mind-numbing simplicity on the assumption that because the rider knows nothing about horses he knows nothing about anything!

I dedicated this book to Terry Thompson and wrote it with his words ringing in my ears. The horses he trains are intended for adults, children, teenagers, professionals, and beginning amateurs. So is this book. He works in a Western saddle but he knows about hunters, jumpers, dressage and park horses and he respects what they can do. Anything they can teach him, he wants to learn. In fact, anything anyone can teach him, he wants to learn! His humour, wit, common sense and honour are qualities I have found in good gamers all over the world. In their various ways they all say, 'We do this for fun. And when it is done right, it is fun!' But I heard it first from Terry Thompson, the master of them all.

9

The First Word

Mounted games are fun but they are not all play. To win and win regularly horse and rider must be prepared to follow a training and conditioning programme that can take years but will produce a safe and competitive horse that will respond at high speeds just as well as a trained polo pony, a trained show jumper or a trained reining horse. With proper preparation, competing in mounted games can add an exciting dimension to anyone's horsemanship if the rider has the dedication to do it right.

Parents and amateur riders should be aware, though, that without proper training games can be very dangerous. Because they are called 'games', the public and a good part of the horse world are convinced that: (a) games classes are just for young children; (b) they are easy and require little preparation; and (c) any fast horse or pony will automatically have a talent for them.

They couldn't be more wrong. For starters, mounted games and gymkhana events are popular all over the world and teenagers, adults and even grandparents are winning them. Pole-bending, barrel-racing and tent-pegging as well as a mass of other events are enjoyed by adult riders from Iran to Canada, the USA, to Australia and New Zealand as well as in the United Kingdom.

As for training and preparation, knowledgeable horsemen have a lot of respect for games riders. They know that gymkhana events may look simple but they are not always easy. On the contrary, many of these games are very sophisticated and require as much or more training than any other horse show class. Pole-bending, for instance, looks like a simple slalom pattern, and it is.

But to do it correctly requires many skills, and the speed at which the pattern must be performed requires fast reactions and great athletic ability in both horse and rider. (If you doubt this, ask a dressage rider how he would like to do five flying changes on the centre line at speed, reverse, and do the same thing again!)

Yet at the end of a horse show so many people throw their young green horses and/or young green children into the games classes just for fun. If it is just for fun, then leave it at that. Hit or miss. Everyone likes a chance to run full out or scramble around on the end of a leading rein while looking for a sack to stand on, and the odd run through the flag race isn't going to do any harm. It is good fun to blow the cobwebs away once in a while and many a good dressage horse or Western pleasure pony has brought home a clutch of ribbons in the egg-and-spoon or pass-the-parcel races (while enjoying himself tremendously).

But if you aren't going to treat the more challenging games seriously, then don't take them seriously. Don't demand skills from yourself and your horse which neither of you has had a chance to learn and practice. And don't punish the pony (or yourself) for not delivering what neither of you has had a chance to develop.

A good games horse or games pony is a highly specialised animal. It is not a good idea to take a good dressage horse, a good show hack or a good Western pleasure horse and *constantly* enter him in games which demand exacting movements performed at high speed (like pole-bending or keyhole race). Some horses and ponies can be all-rounders and they can handle these demands without letting them affect their performance in other areas. But by frequently schooling them for and entering them in advanced speed events, you take the chance of teaching your horse to be too alert, too quick to react to the slightest stimulation. Sometimes a change of tack in these classes keeps the horse from becoming confused. Sometimes a different rider (for different events) helps him keep his two jobs separate.

Just give it a lot of thought before you take a talented specialist in one field and try to make him a specialist in a very different one as well.

1

The Rider

A good games rider does not need to be a prime physical specimen or an exquisite rider but he does need to have good coordination and he must enjoy competition. It does not matter if you are the smallest member of a Pony Club, a businessman who is a little overweight or a housewife who hasn't time to jog or do callisthenics. Just as short, round, funny-looking horses can be very good at games, so too can short, round funny-looking people – if they have some athletic ability and the desire to compete.

Mental attitude has a lot to do with success in this sport. Age or sex cannot make any difference to you when you enter a games class. A winning games rider may find himself riding against a sweet little girl on her pet pony but to that rider, she must be just another competitor. The minute you start feeling sorry for the competition, or get angry at the opposition, that is when the sport will stop being fun; that is when you will make a mistake; and that is when the opposition will beat you. The instant you stop concentrating or get angry instead of aggressive, that is the instant you are in trouble. The winning games rider is the quiet individual who keeps his wits about him, keeps the pressure on the other riders and lets *them* deal with the catching up.

So if you are going to have fun riding in mounted games, you have to have the personality for it. An over-sensitive person who gets upset easily under pressure will not be happy competing in mounted games. Of course we are all a little nervous before a contest no matter how many times we ride, but a games rider has to learn to leave that nervousness at the entry gate and enjoy the game. Luckily the ability to do that is not a matter of age or sex.

There are good child games riders, good lady games riders and a lot of good grandfather games riders.

(Novices are always surprised at how good women and girls are at this sport. Males may have more experience in contact sports and more encouragement to be physically aggressive, but the female of the species can be very successful in this sport too. As long as she has reasonable strength and good coordination, a daughter may ride against her father in barrel-racing or tent-pegging . . . and beat him too!)

The best personality asset a very young games rider can have is a calm, sensible parent. Children entering games often try to produce too much speed too soon, and too many parents encourage them in this. Some parents think it is appealing to see their child running flat out (invariably on a big horse) and they like to think their child is so brave. If that child is without training and proper tack and equipment, or if the horse has not been prepared for the class, the parents have no idea *how* brave that child is.

Riders of all ages must realise that mounted games are not dangerous *per se* as long as the horse and rider are prepared for them. The danger lies in not preparing for a specific class, for which the horse has developed no coordination, is confused and out of control. That situation could lead to a rider being hurt or even killed.

The worst thing that can happen is for a child to get lucky and win a ribbon on his first few times out. Hysteria breaks loose in the family. It's whip and spur and Daddy saying, 'Get out there and win!' The child's technique does not improve – he just aims the pony at the first obstacle and begins thrashing. He hears his parents and friends yelling, and cannot leave that cheering at the entry gate. When he goes into the arena all he can think is: 'Everyone is going to be so disappointed if I don't win.' Very few children can handle that pressure and so they lose their concentration and panic.

A good games instructor gives his student a strategy of how to ride the pattern, tells him to do the best he can, and that's all. The instructor does not put additional pressure on his students. If the horses and riders are calm and know what they are doing, everyone can have a lot of fun, and the trainer, coach or instructor should try to see that they do.

But so many young people and adults new to mounted games

see the maniacs of our sport wildly jerking their horses around and they think this is what you have to do in order to compete. Unfortunately there are still many small-time games riders who believe that if a pony can't do anything else or if a horse is uncontrollable, then he can always be made into a games competitor. A small minority of riders still believe that a games rider just runs his horse madly in all directions and then jerks its head off for a halt. These horses weren't uncontrollable or hysterical to start with but their riders *made* them that way: their riders didn't take the time to learn better technique and they didn't take the time to teach it to their horses. If these uneducated riders compete at a good show, gymkhana or rally, they get beaten badly and they get beaten on technique, not time. The only way we can help these people is through clinics and schools or through books like this one.

Studying your sport is another vital factor in a successful competitor's approach. Go to schools, read books, study articles in horse magazines. Watch how other instructors and riders do things. Always keep your eyes open for any little snippet of information that will help you improve. Study as well as practice is vital to winning and competing safely. The top games riders never feel that they know it all.

Yet no matter how much expertise you have or how much experience or speed, you are still going to lose sometimes. Handling losing is the hardest thing a games rider must face, and it isn't just his own feelings he must deal with. There are the feelings of family, friends, team-mates and, if he is a professional, the public. And the public is very fickle.

A top individual, a top team, or the best flag racer in the village can win everything one week, but the next week might decide to compete on green horses or try a new event just for experience. This time they don't expect to win, and they don't. But if a top rider, a top team or the best rider in the club isn't in the winner's circle every time, there are people who will say, 'He's really down. I think he is losing his touch.' No matter what his level or age a competitor has to learn to accept these remarks and not answer back. It is nevertheless a hard lesson for anyone to learn if he shows and wins a lot. Once a novice starts to win, he feels he must win every time he goes out. He tries to keep his horse and himself at an athletic peak. But no one can stay peaked week after week. Horse and rider are bound to go downhill eventually.

At that point the rider may be tempted to over-ride or over-bit or try some other foolish ploy. A games rider must learn to gauge himself mentally as well as physically. He must constantly think to himself, 'Losing isn't everything. It isn't going to upset me. I've done my share of winning and I will continue to do my share of winning if my knowledge will allow me to do so.'

This ability to ride aggressively without getting angry, to leave the class results in the arena where they belong (instead of brooding for days about the outcome), are the most important attributes of a good games rider. Some people have them naturally; they are born with the right attitude. Others can develop them along with the rest of their mounted games skills and, like many other skills, one is never too young or too old to start.

Begin by attending rallies, gymkhanas or horse shows which feature mounted games. If these activities attract you, join a Pony Club, riding club, 4H (USA) or breed association which offers lessons in these events for its members. If this is impossible in your area, look into lessons with a reputable competitor or trainer who can start you or your child off safely.

It may well be that you have no option but to jump in and test the water alone. If this is the case, study the schedule a few weeks before the show or gymkhana and select one or two events. In the beginning look for classes which do not demand too much of the horse or rider. Musical sacks, ride and lead, 'Simon says', do not demand flying lead changes, 360° turns or other advanced skills. The egg-and-spoon race is another good event where horse and rider can shine without putting undue physical stress on themselves.

Once you have selected the classes, practise them at home and make sure you know the rules. Watch a few events so that you will know what to expect. Enter the smallest show or gymkhana or rally you can find – the bigger the show, the greater the distractions and pressure.

Don't ride to win. All you are doing at this point is market research.

At the end of the day, take a hard look at yourself, your horse and possibly your family. What did you like? What didn't you like? Do you want to get into this sport or was it a once-in-a-life-time experience? Whether it is a local horse show, a Pony Club lesson day for mounted games or a private lesson with a World Champion barrel-racer, you will never know how you really feel about riding in mounted games until you try it for yourself.

From then on it may well be all go.

2

The Horse

The first thing to examine when evaluating a prospective games horse or pony is yourself, the prospective games rider. You are interested; you are enthusiastic. Now go to work on the details. Do you want to compete at small local shows? Are your sights set on the Pony Club and the Prince Philip Cup? Does the Mounted Games Association of Great Britain offer you what you want? How much money do you want to spend on the horse or pony, and how much time and money do you want to spend on competing?

At this point you may already have a horse or pony and want to evaluate his potential. (Many is the solid leading-rein pony who harboured a secret passion and talent for tent-pegging!) Or you may have fourteen horses in the back paddocks and wonder which of them should be trained for games. Finally you may have been promising yourself a horse for years and have just decided that mounted games is the sport for you. In all these cases the criteria are the same. Weigh these factors and decide when looking at individual animals which short-comings you can live with or overcome and which aptitudes and advantages dazzle you.

If you want to earn breed association points (where applicable), you will need a horse or pony registered with that breed association. If not, then papers won't be important to you and you can consider a cross-bred or unregistered animal.

If you are going to compete seriously, it will save time and money in the long run to buy a proven horse or pony with real potential to be a winner instead of getting a youngster to train yourself. However, proven producers of speed can be expensive and if you plan to compete at local level once or twice a month during the summer holidays, or if you are going to enter an event which is not timed (like tent-pegging), then world championship times are not important to you. You could have just as much fun with an average games horse at a more reasonable price.

Most adult-sized games riders prefer a small horse between 14.3 hh and 15.1 hh. Short-coupled with a snappy, athletic body, a good games horse, like a good polo pony, has a comparatively long stride on his short body so he can cover more ground with less effort and time. Agility often comes in small packages but shorter horses have another advantage as well. In tent-pegging, for instance, the rider must lean over and down to pick up the peg with his sabre or lance. The taller the horse, the farther he must lean.

In pole-bending, a long-legged horse can muddle his stride easily and knock down a pole. Here again a compact, fast horse can beat a tall, fast horse. There are 21 feet (6.3m) between each pole, so the smaller the horse you have to put in that space, the more room you have to operate and the more margin for error you have. Of course, there are rare exceptions: if, for example, you want to compete in barrel-racing exclusively, buy a bigger and faster horse; but if you want to compete in barrels *and* poles and other events, then look for a horse between 14.3 hh and 15.1 hh.

Just as adults look for shorter horses so do Pony Club games riders look for shorter ponies, but for an additional reason. The most important factor is that although no pony of 12.2 hh or under may compete in approved games classes by a rider weighing more than 53 kg clothed, no pony over 14.2 hh can compete at all. Another consideration is that in Pony Club competitions, the rider must often vault on and off his mount at speed. The taller the pony, the more difficult this vaulting becomes.

(When North American and Antipodean Youth Division riders in Quarter Horse, Paint, Appaloosa and open games hear about fourteen-year-old riders looking for a games pony between 12.3 hh and 13.1 hh, their reaction is usually a mixture of horror and hilarity. They can be forgiven their preference for bigger horses, though. In their games of pole-bending, barrel-racing, keyhole, etc. no one has to mount or dismount during the class. At least not on purpose.)

Now you would think that a big, long-legged, long-striding

horse would be what we are looking for because games classes are timid events and this type of horse looks like he can beat anything on the straight. He probably can, but remember that games don't involve much straight running. We want a quick, agile sprinter who can turn quickly, and big horses are not always handy horses. When running the poles, his rider has to lift him up and place him at each turn. A smaller horse can gather himself and keep his balance for the quick turns and lead changes.

Rodeo horses, on the other hand, are strictly barrel-racers. Their riders *are* looking for a horse off the sprint racetrack: a big, tall, long-striding horse with some agility. Speed is essential here and getting around the barrel in the best position is secondary to speed. The barrel or cloverleaf pattern is simple with long straight runs between. These riders and horses can afford to sacrifice some manoeuvrability to get the speed they need. Barrel-racing horses usually run once against the clock instead of in heats, horse against horse. So rodeo riders can choose a horse that is a little taller, heavier, speedier and hotter than is needed by a Pony Club member, or a 4Her or MGAGB games rider.

In these clubs and in many breed associations, the horses and ponies often run more than one pattern and they often run them more than once in each class, in a series of heats. In tent-pegging a rider can compete as an individual or as part of a team. When teams run, they can run side by side or with a second interval between a rider and his team-mate. In these events you may have to pass on the big, fast animal if he lacks the ability to repeat his performance time after time or if he hates working close to other horses. In team competitions both horse and rider have to enjoy or at least tolerate working very closely with other competitors. No matter how talented the rider or how nimble the pony, if either is constantly snapping or sniping at lesser lights, they won't last long on a team. In these mounted games the ability to go along and get along is extremely important.

But if the inside (temperament) of a games horse is important, so is the outside. A horse or pony who keeps his hind legs under him, who tracks up, who has well-developed gaskins and hindquarters will be physically able to produce the instant impulsion that games demand. However, we can build up gaskins and hindquarters with work. What we cannot change is the way the neck and head are attached. We look for a horse or pony whose neck comes out of his withers because this indicates that he will run flat and low, rather than bounding up and out.

(We often hear of riders who want a pony 'who enters the ring with his head up, looking around with interest'. Anyone who, when the race begins, has been hit in the face by one of these interested and elevated heads and has consequently had to use a very assertive martingale to keep that head in the working position, soon comes to treasure the heads and necks with a more low-down approach.)

A little stoutness or coarseness on the front legs – whilst still being correct – is certainly no reason to reject a prospective games horse or pony. In fact, many running horses have problems with their legs unless those legs *are* quite stout. A horse should have enough leg and hoof to support his body and should not be refined to the point of fragility.

Many admirers of Appaloosas, Palouse Ponies and Pony of the Americas are attracted to these breeds because of their cold blood and the idea that their temperament can stand the physical and mental pressure of running not once, but many times in a single class.

In short, a good mounted games horse is very like many a good show jumper: not necessary from proven bloodlines, nor blessed with proven conformation but a horse with good coordination and a turn of speed which can be put calmly on 'hold' until his next taxing round without him getting wilder and wilder with each trip.

The biggest mistake you can make in choosing a games mount is to worry too much about speed. If you concentrate on size and speed and ignore temperament and agility, you are going to run into trouble no matter which class you enter. Yes, you have to have speed. Speed is essential in a winner, but with it you have to have a horse with some sense. The tall, squirrel-like horse with nothing but speed will often qualify with the fastest time or win the first event of the day. But often that horse can only run once before losing his head. When he loses his concentration, he loses his balance and then he can be beaten.

Once you have chosen your classes and your club/association, you often have to choose between a mare, a gelding or a stallion.

Each has its advantages and disadvantages. Sometimes the decision (or one of them) is taken out of your hands. The Pony Club will not allow its members to compete on stallions. Other organisations will not allow anyone to do so.

Terry Thompson of the Appaloosa Club in the USA has won many Appaloosa World Championships on stallions and has coached children who have won on Pony of the Americas stallions. He has this advice about stallions and mares:

'Stallions can take the training but they can also bull up easier and turn on you. When you geld a horse you take away a lot of that aggressive personality. The horse stops thinking, "Hey, I want to get out of doing this." Instead a gelding's attitude becomes "Hey, I want to get this job done and go back to my paddock and relax." Many times a stallion will get aggravated with all the work and say to himself, "I'll show him!" And he *can* show you!

'A show horse is more educated than the average horse and therefore he has a more highly developed intelligence. He is smart enough to learn how to do things and so he is going to be smart enough to figure out how to *get out* of doing things too. Stallions seem to have this intelligence in a greater degree than mares or geldings do. Never mind about equal rights. When it comes to physical strength and will-to-win, it takes an extraordinary mare to beat a stallion in a race. Nature gives him the drive, the determination and the power to win.

'But those are not always good qualities to have. For one thing, a stallion can use those qualities against his rider, and for another, he can use them against other horses. It seems like a stallion is always squealing at other horses and challenging them. My studs are good studs but they are always trying it on. Take them to a show and they always have to roll in their stall and risk getting cast or sore. If they are stabled next to a horse they don't like, it seems like they are kicking the stall all week.

'But if a stallion wants to fight when he gets out of sorts, a mare wants to pout when she does. A mare can be moody when she comes into season and then it seems like she is always kicking or snapping at the horses near her. If she has been kicking a lot, then her hocks are sore, and when a horse is sore, she doesn't want to run.'

A gelding is often the best of both worlds. He has the strength of a stallion but without his natural aggression. A gelding goes about his work with a minimum of fuss no matter what day of the month it is, and there is a lot to be said for this attitude if you plan on competing often.

If you want to compete in Prince Philip Cup rallies or earn pony breed association points (where applicable), you will obviously be looking at ponies. 4H (in USA) and MGAGB also sponsor youth games and for the small robust rider there is nothing like a good robust pony. In fact, in small local shows a fast, handy pony can often beat a slower, less agile horse in the open games classes. In open pony classes (as opposed to specific breed classes) these games ponies often lack fierce competition and even a mediocre pony can win his share of ribbons.

But make no mistake, ponies can compete in mounted games successfully and even though ponies often seem to be the most under-trained members of the horse world, they also often have terrific intelligence and ability. Because of their size, most ponies are trained by their child riders so if your family plans on competing games ponies, you must also consider your child's ability and the availability of an experienced adult to guide him in his training.

Clubs, associations, events, sex, breed, rider all seem like a lot of factors to weigh up but many people do not give them enough consideration. When considering a horse or pony for mounted games it is so important to give a lot of thought to the kind of games you want to play and the level at which you want to play them. It is so important to have the right horse (or pony) for the right activity* and if you aren't sure of how deep you want to get into this sport, it is better to start off rather modestly instead of shopping for a proven winner.

Everyone likes the idea of a World Champion or a Prince Philip Cup winner but ask yourself if you (and your family) have the single-minded dedication to be pretty much in constant training. Do you have the time, the transportation and the money to haul your horse around the county for training sessions, and around the country for the big competitions? If you find that you cannot financially or emotionally afford a world-beater, then let someone experienced in your sport find you something you can afford and that fits your needs, or help you have fun with the horse or pony you already have. Everyone wants the best but 'best' means different things to different people.

---

* Some Pony Clubs demand that your child ride just that: a pony. Others encourage the use of small horses. If your child wants to join a particular club or team, be sure that you are both aware of that particular group's requirements.

3

The Specifics

At this point we have narrowed the field considerably. We know the level and type of competition we want to enter. We know the size, the sex and the breed (if that is a factor) of our prospective games horse. We have a good idea of the type of events we will be entering and the kind of people, rules and regulations we will meet there.

However, regardless of the class, there are a few basics that any potential games entry must master before going into specialised training or competition. Both horses and rider must be able to walk, trot and canter in a controlled and balanced fashion. Both must be able to side-pass, two-track, back up and stop. Both must feel confident and comfortable with the flying lead change. The horse must give his head and neck easily to bit or rein pressure and have some sense or feel of the rein.

If there is one weak link in this chain of skills, now is the time to see to it. Look for an instructor, a trainer, an experienced competitor in your sport, a riding school, a clinic – some source of expertise who can help you. Your instructor or coach does not need letters after his name or a string of ribbons on the wall. What he must have is the ability to teach you and your horse what you need to know. He also needs to have some knowledge of mounted games and a sympathetic attitude toward them.

(There is a small, narrow-minded segment of the horse community that has a bad attitude to mounted games and the people who compete in them. Unless you are very strong-minded, you will spend your lessons with these people just trying to justify your existence and convince them that all games riders are not hooligans. Every lesson with this sort of coach is going to feature him sneering at you and you muttering under your breath. Nobody needs this kind of atmosphere. Avoid it.)

Take a little time to find a teacher who likes you, your horse, and likes the idea of smoothing someone's path into mounted games. Explain what your problem areas are ('I cannot recognise a lead change,' 'Please look at my side-pass and see if this horse is stiff to one side, or is it me? What can I do about it?') Private lessons are more expensive than group ones but for pinpointing a problem and solving it quickly, they are the cheapest way to go.

If we are going to have a good games horse and want to be able to ride him well, we gave to spend some time on the basic skills. The time it takes to make a good, safe games horse and a good, safe games rider is the most underestimated thing in the horse sport. It may take many months of basic training before we can even walk through a cloverleaf or keyhole pattern and we have to have that training mastered.

Once we have established our horse's and our own educational background, we can begin looking at our horse closely and testing him on what he knows. The first thing to consider is how, as the Western riders say, 'the horse packs his bridle'. A games horse must yield to the bit and rein. If he resists and shakes his head, he will spend more time fighting his rider and getting off balance and he will never make up that lost time. It is not enough that he, for instance, side-passes. If he is fighting with his head, resisting the bit while he side-passes, we do not want him. If he is unresponsive we do not want him. Because if he is a trained horse and still fighting the bit, he will never get over it, and if we cannot control the head, we have little hope of controlling the horse - especially at speed.

After we have checked out this basic training, we can try the horse at faster speeds. Stand him at an imaginary line and ask him to push off into a canter. Stop him and let him rest a moment. Now try again. Give him a hard cue forward to see if he leaves low and fast.

A good games horse should move like a dragster – a hot rod – low in front to spring forward. His head should stay low. A games horse, like any other sprinter, cannot leave the starting line high. If he leaps up instead of forward, he will lose distance and time. Ideally we are looking for a horse that is fast off the line, almost dropping to his knees when he takes off. If the horse does not stay low, if his head and neck carriage is just a little high but everything else is right, the horse can still be a good average games competitor or we can work on other facets of his performance to make up for his failings here.

Now we check the lead changes, and by that we mean flying lead changes. We want a horse that changes leads naturally (preferably hind lead first) and in balance because balance is the essence of a good games horse. If he cannot maintain his balance, he cannot handle his speed. This is why we are very careful to keep the horse upright and straight when asking for a lead change. Suddenly throwing your horse onto the opposite bend will often effect a lead change (usually only in front) but it also throws the horse off balance.

In pole-bending a balanced lead change at every pole isn't just important – it's imperative. In throwing a horse onto a lead change a rider often throws him into the pole.

So far we have checked our horse's form at the starting line, his balanced lead change in both directions, his ability to change leads on command and now we want to look at his willingness to stop.

This is very important. We need a horse that *wants* to stop and stand still.

This may sound like an odd trait in a horse whose job will be to move as fast as he can, but 'looking for whoa' has its advantages. In the first place, if there are two horses running against each other in a heat and one jumps the line before the starter signals, some associations disqualify that horse. In the second place, although games are speed events, the rider often has to check or half-halt his horse to position him. The rider can use that half-halt to let the horse gather himself if he is a little off stride between the poles or barrels, just like a show jumper between jumps. Finally, in many team events like tent-pegging, presentation and drill make up a good portion of the possible points to be earned. The horse or pony dancing in place or wanting to bolt off in all directions instead of waiting quietly for orders, will cost his ride and his team dearly.

These little details in selection and training are often overlooked by enthusiastic games riders who want to get into real competition **right now**. But they are details that can cost them victory if they are ignored.

4

The Basic Equitation

Mounted games is one of the few areas of competition which allows the Western rider to hold his reins in both hands and the English rider to hold his reins in one hand. Every rider has a choice. However, as soon as they hear this, riders of both persuasions assume that the rest of their usual rules of equitation do not apply either. Wrong. If anything, the usual rules of horsemanship and the usual standards of excellence apply even more in games because the sharp turns, the speed and the sudden stops leave very little margin for error.

So now that we have spent some time checking and testing the games horse, it is time to check and test the games rider. All the skills and good advice you have picked up so far in your riding career still apply when riding in mounted games, but there are many ways of applying them. Each of those applications has its advantages, so examine them and judge for yourself which apply to you, your event and your particular horse or pony.

For instance, maintaining a balanced position (the rider's ear, hip bone and heel in alignment) is just as important to a games rider as it is to any other horseman. It is crucial to a games rider not only to assume that correct position but to maintain it while moving at speed, turning and stopping quickly. If he tips forward or falls back, the games rider can throw his horse off balance or break his concentration, which leads to losing time or making errors.

For example, if the rider is caught off guard and falls back in the saddle when his horse lunges forward at the starting line, that rider has two undesirable options. He can regain his position and get in motion with his horse by pulling himself forward by the reins. This signals the horse to stop or slow down which costs time. The other option is to thrash his way back into balance by using his legs and twisting his body which throws the horse off balance (which also loses time).

So we can see that games riding is very much like speed jumping. In both competitions the horse is turning and twisting quickly, and a secure leg position and a balanced, secure seat is what keeps the rider in place and prevents him from interfering with his horse's performance. (If the rider's feet are too far forward, he will always be falling back on the cantle and will have a hard time getting forward to pass objects to his team-mates, pick up pegs, or simply maintain his position over his horse's centre of gravity so the horse can easily maintain his own balance and forward movement. If the rider carries his feet and legs too far back, he will always be falling onto his horse's neck, he will always be off balance and he will be throwing his horse off balance as well.)

So riding with your feet underneath you, with a flexed ankle, is not just a matter of looking good. A correct, balanced position is what keeps you, the rider in balance. And that balance affects how well your horse performs and how well you score.

Maintain yourself in this position with your calves and balance. In a quick start on a quick turn you may need to hold yourself in position. Use your calves and lower legs, not your knees, to do it. This gives you a larger gripping surface than if you just clamped your knees on your pony's sides. Let your knees relax and 'breathe' at all times. Hold, not grip, your pony's sides with your calves and lower legs: it is easier and more effective.

To check your position, to see if you are correctly balanced, stand in your stirrups with your knees slightly flexed. Let your weight go down through your calves to your feet and heels. Let your ankles flex. If you tip forward, your feet are too far behind the girth. If you fall back and sit down, your feet are too far forward. With your feet directly beneath you, your knees slightly bent, your ankles flexed, your calves holding the horse's sides, and most of your weight in your heels, you are ready to ride close to the saddle, leaning slightly forward.

Now a Western equitation seat, a dressage seat, puts the rider in the middle of his saddle. He is sitting straight with a long leg.

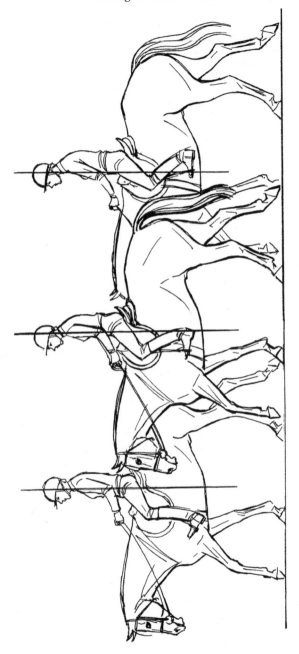

Whether riding English or Western maintain a balanced position to keep from being thrown forward or back. If your ear, hip bone and heel are in alignment, you are in a winning position.

However, a gymkhana position is closer to that of a show jumper. Keep the hip and heel alignment you use in equitation and dressage but ride with a slightly shorter stirrup and be prepared to lean forward slightly from the hip when you ask for more extension. The slightly shorter stirrup and firm calf contact hold the games rider in place and give him greater security as his horse twists and turns, starts and stops quickly. With a secure and balanced position the games rider's hands and arms can act independently and with greater finesse.

At this point we want to test our position just as we tested our horse. Assuming this position is good at the halt or walk can we maintain this balance and poise at speed? Trot and canter 20-metre circles in your games position. Reverse at the trot. Ride 20-metre circles at the canter and then push the circle out to 40 metres and extend the horse into something faster but still controlled. Ask your teacher, trainer, a close friend or parent to watch and see if you maintain this balance and position. Ask them to see if you have actually increased the speed.

(Because most riders start off with formal riding lessons and because of the great popularity of dressage and equitation classes, these riders often spend years riding contentedly but without experiencing speed. In many parts of the world hunting and cross-country gallops are out of the question. In big city recreation areas, even cantering is frowned upon. So it is not unreasonable to find experienced riders who have no idea what a real gallop or extended canter feels like. Getting used to speed and feeling at home with it requires practice in a safe environment.)

To help maintain your balance and correct position at all gaits and speeds, hold the reins in both hands for maximum control over the horse and your position. Use a single, short, joined rein for this instead of the traditional split reins, or a romal in Western, or the longer English reins joined by a buckle. If you cannot find a short single rein, tie a knot in your reins and work from there. Shortening and lengthening the reins by the traditional method takes too long when decisions must be made quickly. Sometimes the horse must be extended or collected in one stride. To do this efficiently, take up a good contact with your shortened reins and just extend or shorten your arms to give the horse the freedom to run at a longer stride, or bring your

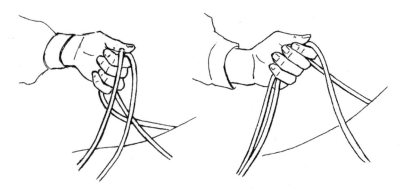

Western reining, Texas style. With the split reins the rider can put one finger through the reins if he chooses. The free hand is held in a natural position with the elbow flexed gently and the hand either on the thigh or carried near the belt buckle.

hands back to check or shorten his stride.

It is a fact of life in the horse world that the general public tends to under-rate games riders. The uninformed tend to think that because the horse is a games horse, his rider can just sit there and go to sleep. Nothing could be farther from the truth! In actual fact, good mounted games riders have an exceptionally sophisticated technique. Even the simplest pattern requires many adjustments in stride and position, and those adjustments must be made very quickly. Also there are many variations in personal style, each with its own reason behind it.

For instance, there are at least three main ways to simply sit in the saddle when riding the barrel-racer's cloverleaf pattern. Some people ride the entire pattern in two-point contact: weight in the feet, holding with the calves but riding close to the saddle rather than in it. Others cross the starting line in that position but, a stride before turning each barrel, these riders sit right down in the saddle and drive with their seat as well as using steady pressure of their legs. In this way they have a little more push and control and some horses need it. When their horse begins the big straight run between the barrels and when coming home, these riders lean forward and out of their saddle to help the horse extend his stride. Finally there are many successful riders who sit deep in the saddle for the whole run, driving and holding with

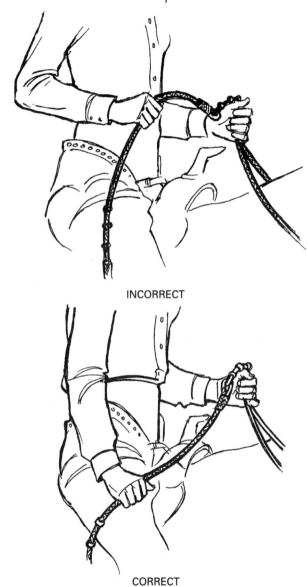

INCORRECT

CORRECT

California reining – a style of Western riding which uses a joined rein called a romal. In this style the rider's free hand holds the romal and rests on the rider's thigh.

33

their seat and legs every inch of the way for maximum control and push.

There are many factors that go into riding strategy. As size and weight of the rider are two of these factors, let's take a close look at how one teenage boy adjusted his style of riding to fit his conformation and that of his pony.

Just as there is a magic moment when boots are absolutely broken in, so there is a magic moment when a Youth Division or Pony Club rider is in perfect proportion with his pony *and* has the strength, timing and experience to make the partnership a winning one. It seems like all systems are **go** and the sky is the limit. There is nothing to compensate for and nothing to overcome.

Then Nature takes over.

The child rider may be a child in years but soon, in size and shape, adult life is just around the corner. As he puts on weight and inches, the rider's margin for error becomes smaller and smaller and sometimes it seems like the pony is working under a handicap instead of under a rider. Some clubs have a rider weight/pony height limit or ratio that must be observed. Other organisations just let Nature take its course when time penalties begin to separate the men from the boys and the women from the girls.

Seventeen-year-old Dee Bowers faced this problem when he was competing his Pony of the Americas stallion Lannan's Siri Superdot Minute Man. When Dee went on to university, Minute Man went on to Australia to be one of the most famous sires of their Palouse breed. But in the last years of Dee's eligibility as a pony rider, they made national names for themselves on the United States Pony of the Americas gymkhana circuit.

'Minute Man and I had a number of things going against us. I was tall and weighed 150 lbs [67.5kg] so in games which were flat-out running, I could never expect to do well. I would be lucky to get a fourth or fifth place.

'I realised that if I wanted us to be successful in gymkhana we would have to make our time on the turns instead of the straightaway. We could be competitive in classes like pole-bending and barrel-racing. In order to make time on the turns, Minute Man was going to have to be extremely accurate and we were going to have to gain that accuracy pretty much on our own, because our second big problem was that we couldn't get a lot of coaching.

'I know that it is exciting to go charging around all the time, going as fast as you can, but from the beginning I had to stress accuracy instead and concentrate on the details every minute. For instance, if you are bar-rel-racing, you have to make a complete 180° turn on every barrel. The rider who doesn't practice this correctly gets half way around his barrel and then forgets the rest of the turn because he is so busy thinking about the next barrel. These incomplete turns throw the horse off balance and it takes seconds for him to regain it.

'If I found myself cutting my turns short, I'd correct myself in practice. Minute Man and I would go to the barrel, stop, turn around the barrel, stop, and then go on to the next barrel. This stopping and checking taught both of us to make the complete turn. If you make yourself and your pony stop and think of each step at the beginning, if you break every pattern down into its basic parts, the turns or whatever will be second nature to you when you actually begin to race.

'Another common error in barrel racing is allowing the horse to weave as he runs from barrel to barrel. No matter what the game is, the shortest distance between two points is a straight line and it is up to the rider to make sure his horse is running that straight line. Besides, if the horse is weaving, the chance for him to be off stride is greater, especially with a taller, heavier rider.

'It makes no sense for a rider of any size to just run his pony up to a barrel and then all of a sudden yank the reins for a stop or turn. Once my pony had learned his patterns and could turn on the speed when he had to, I realised that the next step toward better times was up to me. I had to work on developing a sense of giving cues for the turns around the bar-rels. I learned that it is best to give a cue or aid one or two strides before the barrel or turn so that my pony would have time to prepare himself.

'He had to be balanced going into his turns and he had to be aware of what he was going to do once he got there. So when Minute Man was running between the barrels, I was always out of the saddle, standing in my stirrups, but keeping close to the saddle. As long as I could hold myself quiet and steady, it was easier for him to move. As soon as I wanted to prepare him for a turn, I sat down and gave him a slight check or half-halt. When we began turning the barrel, I would be completely down in the saddle, really using my outside leg to bend him around the turn.

'And I always looked toward the next barrel. That is something we games riders can learn from the show jumpers. Always look on to the next point instead of down at the point you are at now.

'Once we mastered the aids for turns, I concentrated on riding the whole pattern, putting all the steps together. The rider's legs are crucial on turns but they important on the straightaway too. A games rider has to be aware that there is a big difference between using his legs and not just drumming and flapping them on the pony's sides. When a jockey is riding in a race, he isn't moving in any way that would throw his horse off stride. He is so in time with his horse that it looks like he isn't moving at all! You see these little kids (no matter what size they are) flapping their legs and yelling "Go! Go!" All they are doing is interfering with their pony and slowing him down.

'I tried to stay as still as I could in the saddle. I found that if I just closed my legs on his sides firmly and didn't move, my pony could go much faster.

'Gymkhana is a matter of training the pony, not over-powering him. If you keep this in mind, games aren't going to ruin your show horse any more than teaching him any other new thing will. The main idea is never to push for speed in training. If you have your pattern down, you'll find that when the pony needs to run, he can.

'As Minute Man worked faster and faster times, I tried to concentrate more on the starts. Getting into the ring and across the starting line properly takes a lot of schooling, both for the horse and for the rider. It is against the rules of most organisations to run into the arena, but some clubs will let you start trotting or cantering once the pony's hindquarters are clear of the gate. This is foolish. The pony has no chance to see the first obstacle until he is on top of it. He has no chance to see what is he is supposed to do and he has no time to prepare himself.

'Besides, there are plenty of instances when running from the gate won't save any time at all. In pole-bending, for example, it is important to start straight. If your horse runs from the gate, he is running on a slant, running a longer path and it will take a hard, time-consuming turn to get him into the correct position to start the pattern.'

Now all these points apply to the child-sized rider as well as to the adult-sized one. The interesting thing is that they are brought to our attention by a boy who worried that he might be too big for his pony. He wasn't as far as mounted games were concerned, but the planning and strategy he brought to his career in pony-oriented mounted games is useful to everyone taking up this sport. Keep it in mind.

Attacking one problem often leads to success in all sorts of other areas, some of them only slightly related to the original problem.

5

Additional Skills

So mounted games not only require a willing and athletic pony, they also require a willing and athletic rider who asks as much of himself as he does of his mount. In these events there is no place for the solid, stolid rider whose only role is to hold a pretty position in the saddle. In mounted games the rider is expected to do his share of running, leaning and turning, and many classes demand pony and rider to run side by side while carrying eggs, socks, buckets or other riders.

To find out what sort of gymnastics you have let yourself (and your pony) in for, turn to your show programme or association rule book for specific class requirements. However, no matter what the individual event requires, rest assured that the following skills will come in handy during the course of your mounted games career.

Leading

Some clubs and breed associations encourage their members to show their horses and ponies in hand as well as under saddle, and so these competitors have a head start on everyone else when they are required to run and lead. However, even these paragons of virtue become alarmed when they are running beside not only their own leader but also a mass of other entries as well.

So even if you and your pony have considerable experience at showing in hand, it might be wise to hone and polish your skills – as well as expand them – before going into games competition. First, let's just assume that your pony will walk willingly more or less beside you. To bring him up to gymkhana standard, assemble your pony, a halter, a long, soft lead rope and a friend. Don't be tempted to use a nylon lead strap as it will burn your hands if the pony gets carried away. Find a nice jogging surface with no holes, rocks or tall grass to distract the pony or trip up the leader. Don't use tarmac as it is slippery for fast work and you and the pony may fall down.

Lead the pony around in **big** 20-metre circles. Walk at the pony's left side in an area between his shoulder and his head. Do not snuggle up to the pony. Working too close is a good way to get your feet stepped on. Play out the lead rope and walk about one or two feet (half a metre) away from the pony. This extra space and a little slack in the line allow him to use his head and neck to keep his balance.

If the pony lags behind, cluck, chirp, growl or use whatever command you have chosen to mean 'Get up!' You are allowed to talk in games classes and the voice is the most under-rated natural aid in the horse world. Don't ignore it. It works! If your voice command fails, ask a friend to encourage the pony from behind by clucking, clapping or judiciously using a lunge whip. When the pony moves along to your satisfaction, tell him what a great pony he is, but don't stop moving while you do it.

When it is time to step up the pace, don't try to drag the pony faster. Don't stop and stare at the pony (because that makes him stop and stare back at you). Don't carry a long whip in your outside hand and reach around behind to tap the pony forward. (When you turn away to use the whip, you will pull the pony's head toward you and his hindquarters will swing out. It puts him off course and off balance. When he feels the whip he will swing further away from you and you will have to stop and rearrange him and the whole message will get lost.) Ask a friend or parent to use the whip to tap the pony forward.

By now this pony is getting the idea that he is supposed to keep up with you. You set the pace and he matches it. Soon you will not have to signal him to move faster when you move faster. He will simply know what is expected of him. Now you can start jogging, encouraging him with your voice. You may want to take a few jogging steps in place and say 'Ready' or something similar to give him time to prepare himself. Then jog out slowly. Encourage him by saying nice enthusiastic things to him as you two jog along. Don't pull on the lead rope. Don't stare at him. Give him enough slack in the rope so he can move freely.

Try the same exercise in the other direction.

Try it in a straight line. Take a few walking steps, jog once or twice saying 'Ready', and then jog out smartly, giving him lots of pats and encouragement when you halt at the end of your run. Gradually build up your speed but always keep the pony beside you. Always give him the warning before you break into a jog or run. (Don't just peel off from a dead halt and snap his head off.) Work this running and jogging in hand into your daily routine; trot in from his pasture or on his way out to play.

What we are establishing here is what every well-trained dog learns very early – match your speed to that of your leader. If he walks, you walk. If he runs, you run. When you both are fit and comfortable, try your leading work with different props. For instance, jump into a feed sack and hop along beside your pony. Trot over poles on the ground. Take a few low jumps together. Not only will your pony's track work improve, yours will too!

Flying Dismount

There is nothing more satisfying after a good work-out than the good old Pony Club dismount: feet out of the stirrups, right hand on the pommel, left hand on the pony's neck, lean forward and swing your right leg over the back of the saddle. Land on your feet with a spring and bounce in your ankles. (If you land flat-footed with a stiff knee and ankle, especially in the winter, it will feel like you have broken every bone in your foot. You won't have done. It will just *feel* like it.)

Practice this dismount at the halt, then at the walk. Then try it at a trot. Push out strongly with your hands so you will land away from the pony and not under his feet. As you land, take a few running steps forward to maintain your momentum. (This also keeps you from falling backward and sitting down hard on the ground.) Keep your hand on the rein so you and the pony are still connected.

Every Pony Club member learns this terrific way of getting out of the saddle but it often comes as a revelation to Western riders

The step-by-step approach to a flying dismount can be practised first at the halt, then the trot and on up to the canter. Remember, you are getting the pony used to this manoeuvre as well as yourself.

(unless they have done calf-roping). Hitting the ground running is much faster than stepping out of the saddle and it is also a lot of fun. Just remember, if you are using a Western saddle, don't lean too far forward or you may hook your belt over the saddle horn and spend the rest of the class dangling there.

Vaulting on

Vaulting or swinging onto a moving horse is very much like plaiting tails. Most people say they *can't* do it but what they mean is that they don't want to take the time to learn to do it easily. Yes, it will take practice and it will take time to build up your strength and coordination. But, like plaiting and rising to the trot and doing flying changes, vaulting is **worth the effort**.

Although stockmen and jockeys often practice vaulting onto a fence rail (it gets them into the habit of landing very lightly in the saddle) the easiest way to start is on a trotting pony. If you have a choice begin on the shortest pony you can find and then build up to the taller models. Don't try vaulting onto a walking or standing pony. It is much harder.

Unlike dismounting, it is easier to begin vaulting on a pony from the trot. Jog beside him and then swing up.

Trot along beside your trotting pony, both of you facing forwards. Carry your reins in your left hand and rest that left hand on the pony's crest. Reach across the saddle with your right arm and take hold of the saddle flap on the other side.

When the pony's left front foot hits the ground, jump with both feet together and as you go up and forward, swing your leg over the saddle. Bear your weight on your right arm and shoulder.

After the first try it will be very clear to you why you chose the shortest pony you could find. You will also understand why those tall, willowy Prince Philip Cup riders choose short ponies. Like riding a bicycle, ice-skating and skateboarding, vaulting onto a pony can make you look magnificent once you have mastered it and like a complete fool while you are practising. Just keep practising every chance you get and soon you will be able to swing up onto everything in the county.

Neck-reining

If the Pony Club member feels somewhat superior to the Western rider when it comes to vaulting onto and off a moving pony, so the Western rider is permitted a smile the first time he sees an 'English' rider trying to neck-rein. Because a good cutting horse makes it look so easy, many people believe that you can just get on any horse, maintain a light rein contact, let the rein fall against the horse's neck and he will naturally begin turning on a dime, giving back a nickle change. It ain't necessarily so. Neck-reining, like everything else, takes time, training and patience but it is a wonderful skill worth having as any cowboy, cavalry officer or games rider can tell you.

Begin by taking up a light contact on your pony's mouth and hold the reins in one hand, over and in front of the pommel. In a Western gymkhana you are allowed one finger between the reins. Or you can try the Pony Club method of holding the palm of your hand downwards with your wrist flexed. Do not carry your hand any higher than you would if you were holding the reins in both hands.

Walk your pony forward and to turn him to the right, push with your left leg and bring the rein across his neck to the right.

If he doesn't understand, create a little pressure on the right rein to reinforce your aids. As he turns right, tell him what a clever pony he is and give him a pat with your free hand as he walks along.

Now try a left turn, pushing with your right leg and bringing the rein across his neck to the left. Pat him and praise him. Try riding zig-zags down the long side of the arena, always remember to work both ways round the arena and not just in the direction that is easier. Practise every time you ride your pony.

As you begin working at the faster gaits, resist the temptation to give stronger rein aids. If the pony is not moving off the rein as easily as you would like, use a firmer leg aid or, if you feel that the pony is a little confused, take your reins back into both hands. Draw the rein across his neck and reinforce this aid with a light direct rein aid on the opposite side.

Sound easy? It is. But there are a few traps to avoid. One of them is holding your rein hand too high. This comes from watching too many 1940s Western movies. Your rein hand belongs in the same place as it does when direct reining: over and in front of the pommel. Any higher and you are pulling up on the pony's mouth, which causes him pain and confusion.

The second trap is reining too hard. It usually happens when the rider forgets to use his leg aids and relies totally on his reins. The pony doesn't react fast enough so the rider brings the rein over the pony's neck and down the other side in the heat of the moment. This twists the pony's head up and out to the side. Apart from causing pain and confusion, the rider has given a hard direct rein aid to do the opposite of what he intended.

So keep in mind that your legs are more than fifty per cent of the neck-reining aid and don't forget to use them. Keep practising and do not be afraid to reinforce your neck-rein aid with a direct rein if the pony is confused. Give your pony and yourself plenty of time to learn these new skills.

Stopping

After years of trying to achieve smooth downward transitions, it is hard to get used to asking for an instant stop. Gliding gently through the gears to a quiet smooth halt is the goal of every rider and there always seems to be something faintly illegal about power brakes. We see the idiots of our sport yanking their horses to a screaming halt and suddenly we want to rethink the whole idea of mounted games. Rest assured that it does not have to be that way.

You can build a stop just like you did neck-reining and vaulting. It will take a little time and a little patience but, like the rest of your mounted games skills, a snappy halt will come in handy in competition and in your everyday riding too. Here is where the stop starts.

Remember all those riding lessons when the instructor called, 'Prepare to walk . . . and . . . walk on. Prepare to trot. . . and . . . trot on.'? That 'prepare' gave you a warning of what was coming up and it gave you time to get ready for it. You could shorten or lengthen your reins, sit down in your saddle, make all sorts of adjustments to get ready for the next thing.

You are going to do your pony the same kindness. Before we even think of stopping, decide on a word that is going to warn him that a hard, fast halt is coming up. It can be, 'Steady . . . steady . . . **halt.**' It can be, 'Stop . . . stop . . . **now.**' It can be 'Vanilla . . . **fudge!**' It can be anything you like but once you decide on it, that is the warning and command you must *always* use. It is not fair to change the signals halfway through the class.

Now set up a cone or a barrel or some other landmark and declare that you will stop at that point. One inch further and you are over the cliff or in the monster's jaws. Now start walking toward the point. A few strides away give your warning in a firm low voice that means business. Sit down. Close your legs. Lean back slightly from the hip. Give a firm rein signal to stop and the instant you feel your pony lock down to a halt, give the reins slightly. Then ask again with the reins (legs and seat are still in the halt position). Stop at your marker and count to five. Then move off quietly at the walk with lots of pats and kind words.

Do this several more times and then go off and do something else.

When you both feel confident at the walk, move up to the trot. When you have conquered that, try the canter. Always stop on your marker. Always give the warning. Always give a little with

To bring your horse's legs under him in a balanced halt, prepare him and then close your legs.

the reins when you feel the pony lock down. Always wait a few seconds in the halt before moving off.

Then vary the pattern. Canter down and halt, but this time turn quickly, race back and halt then count and *then* walk off. These variations will keep your pony attentive and listening to you.

As you progress in this programme you will find that you have to use less and less rein to get a fast halt. You may find that all you have to do is give the warning, sit back, close your legs and touch the rein. Rodeo horses have been working on those aids for generations. There is no reason why your pony cannot do it too.

Well, actually there is a reason. Lack of sensitivity in the rider can cause problems. An example of this is the rider who gives the warning signal, and then keeps pulling on the reins as hard and as high as he can until the horse grinds to a halt, usually with his head in the air and his eyes on stalks. To avoid this situation learn to feel with your seat and legs when the horse is starting to stop. You will feel a 'locking down' in the hindquarters (both yours and his). At that point give with the rein slightly (as a way of saying thank you) and then ask again. Your seat and legs can give a very strong halt signal without hurting the horse, but your reins should give and take firmly but instantly when asking for a fast halt.

Passing Skills

Until now we have been discussing what the pony (and the horse as well) needs in the way of specialised skills, but the rider must be prepared too. In addition to being the captain and navigator of the ship, he is also required to be part of the crew. In many games you will be called upon to put the flags in barrels, pass batons, and deposit all sorts of articles in all sorts of places. Although the articles may change from game to game, the **passing skills** remain the same.

No matter what you are passing or carrying, the most important thing to remember is not to look at it. Don't look at your hands. Don't look at the ground. Look where you are going and where you are going to the put your flag, or cup, or whatever. For instance, as you round the first barrel, turn your head and look at the second one. As you approach the first pole, look on to the second one. Throw your heart not only over, but around the corner as well.

The only way to practise passing things is to pass them. You cannot practise this skill on your own and that is a very good thing. Practising with a friend not only hones your skills but it also gets your pony used to dealing with other ponies at close quarters.

As usual, begin at the walk and keep on at the walk until the correct grip and technique are second nature to all members of the team. Only then move up to the faster gaits. (If you have to think of how you are going to grasp the tea cup or sock then you should keep on practising at the walk until handling your particular prop is instinctive.)

Always use the correct equipment. If you are required to pass a baton, make a baton. Don't use a corn stalk or a potato masher. The closer you can duplicate all the equipment and sounds of a real gymkhana, the less there will be to distract you, your pony and your team when it counts. If you think that the loudspeaker will be a problem, bring along a portable radio to your practice sessions and tune it in to the most rousing music you can find.

But if the surroundings present a problem to the rider, so does the equipment. It often seems like every object requires its own special grip. Pick up a cup by the rim, not the handle. Hold a bottle with your hand facing forward, then turn it in your hand to drop it from the top or pass it neck foremost. When dropping flags into cones, hold the flag like a sword. When picking a flag out of a cone grasp it with your palm forward and thumb on top.

For those ponies and riders embarking on a career in Pony Club games or any gymkhana rider who wants to perfect his technique, two books are worth having constantly at your side: Toni Webber's *How to Win at Gymkhana* (Ashford, Southampton, 1989) and *Gymkhanas and Rally Games* (a Pony Club publication, Threshold Books, London, 1989). Besides giving a wealth of information on every facet of organising and presenting a gymkhana or rally, both books describe every way of picking up, putting down and aiming the various implements you face at a Pony Club competition.

One of the most popular items on any horse show games list or Pony Club rally is the flag race. This old favourite is found in Canada, Australia and all parts of the world where games riders meet. Because of its universality, it deserves special attention.

Sometimes the flag is handed to the rider and he is sent on his way to deposit it in a holder, pick up another flag and carry it on. In other versions, the rider must ride to the first flag, snatch it out of a holder and proceed. This is only one of the instances where you will be very glad you spent all that time halting and backing at barrels and teaching your horse to check or half-halt on command. That pause will give you a chance to snatch up your flag without hauling your pony all over the arena hoping he will stop. Toni Webber recommends taking the flag 'with the palm facing forwards, thumb uppermost'. Reach forward to grab it out of the barrel. This will give you a little margin for

With the flag turned in your hand, approach the second barrel on a straight line.

error if you miss your first grab.

As you approach the second barrel, come in on a straight line, angling toward the barrel. Turn the flag in your hand (en route to the barrel) so the stick end is pointing toward the barrel. Some riders like to pause and put it in the holder carefully. Others like to toss it in on their way past, rather like throwing darts. The 'dart thrower' doesn't lose any time by breaking his speed but if he misses, he misses the class. Know yourself, know your pony, and make your own decision.

6

The Bits and Pieces

The tack and equipment a trainer uses in perfecting all these skills in his training sessions is pretty much his own business. Some riders swear by the bosal for basic training. Others prefer a snaffle bit. Some use leg bandages at all times, other use boots, and still others use nothing at all on their horse's legs. At home what you put on your horse or pony is a matter of personal preference and personal style.

But when you go into competition then you must obey that particular competition's rules regarding tack and equipment. Not only can those rules change from year to year but they can also differ within an organisation (as to how those rules are interpreted). Having said this, let's take a look at some artificial aids used when training for and competing in mounted games. They may help you solve or prevent some problems that have appeared as your training progresses.

Leg protection is a way of life for many horses participating in mounted games. If they are lungeing or riding, jumping or working at speed, their riders feel it is better to be safe than sorry. Hitting cones, hitting barrels, hitting pegs, over-reaching or bruising can happen at any time and while leg protection for your horse or pony is not required, it is something you may want to consider. The faster you travel, the tighter you turn, the more you want to investigate this type of preventive medicine.

The options and their supporters are legion. Sharon Camarillo, who has been competing and training barrel-racers for more than twenty years, uses over-reach (or bell) boots and combination boots on her horses' front legs and skid boots (see diagram) on

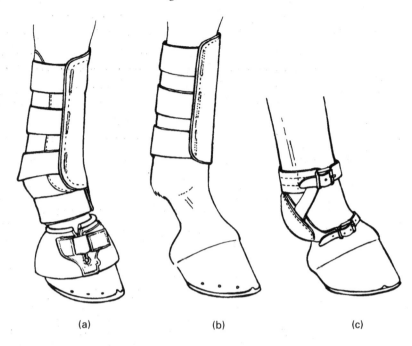

(a) Bell boots and combination boots. (b) Splint boots. (c) Skid boots.

the hind legs. Terry Thompson, the Appaloosa all-rounder, uses splint boots (see diagram) to be on the safe side. Some riders prefer to use bandages. If you do, just make sure they are properly applied and securely fastened at the side. A bandage that is too tight or improperly fastened can cause lameness and one that is loose and unwinding can cause much worse.

Sheepskin girth covers are popular wherever mounted games are played. These woolly sleeves absorb sweat and do a lot to prevent girth sores. Girth covers come in virtually any length for Western, English, pony or horse riders and can even be made at home if you have the necessary sheepskin. If you have some left over, you may want to make a cover for your horse's breastplate as well.

A breastplate is required when tent-pegging and recommended for *any* horse or pony whose conformation encourages the saddle to slip backwards. Along with Western breastplates we have several other variations on this theme: the Aintree race breastplate, the polo breastplate, the stockman's breastplate and the hunting breastplate. For mounted games, a stockman's three-piece breastplate or a hunting breastplate are the best. These styles allow great freedom for the shoulders to move, and all three allow for a martingale to be attached.

Martingales come into the category of 'better to have it and not need it than to need it and not have it'. Western riders call them 'tie-downs', but that is just a turn of phrase rather than a statement of purpose. No matter what you call them, these single or Y-shaped straps, when correctly fitted, come into play only when the horse throws his head up above the line of control. The martingale ('standing', which works on the cavesson noseband, and 'running', which works through the reins) encourages the horse to keep his head down in the working position and many riders use it on every horse they ride as a safety precaution.

Professional and experienced horsemen may or may not use a whip when training but the sensible ones never like to see a whip used in competition. Most riders would like to see whips declared illegal in *all* gymkhana classes (not just in Pony Club). This is because although whips are not in themselves dangerous, they do create dangerous situations. They encourage carelessness in riders and souring of horses that comes from that carelessness.

Ninety-nine per cent of the time, using a whip in competition does more harm than good. Most riders (no matter what their age) use a whip like a car's accelerator. These riders think that the harder they use a crop, the more speed they will get. Actually in swinging a crop, these riders are throwing their horse off stride and thereby losing time. The horse is flinching from the pain and slowing down to get away from the blow.

Besides, if a horse is already giving all he has (and it is safer to assume that he is) then he will consider the whip as a punishment for doing his best. The horse thinks, 'Hey, I'm running as fast as I can and I'm getting hit. I'm not sure I like this. I'm certainly not going to be so eager to go in and run that pattern next time if this is what is going to happen!'

Soon that horse will start refusing to enter the arena or he will shy in all directions trying to get away from the whip. At that point the rider thinks he has a control problem and puts a stronger bit in the horse's mouth, which only compounds the problem. Sometimes, though, a horse or pony is reluctant to enter the arena because he is calling his rider's bluff. If the noise bothers the horse, try putting big handfuls of cotton wool in his ears. If, on the other hand, the horse is just trying it on, then you will have to use your legs and wits and let him know that he *is* going in there and he *is* going to behave himself.

But these are rare instances. What really causes souring in mounted-games horses and ponies is the improper use and abuse of the horse or pony. And that means too much work on one pattern at top speed, or it means that the animal is being pressured with the bit or the whip. Correctly trained horses or ponies do not go sour on games if they know how to do the pattern and if they have been brought on carefully so they do not hurt their mind or their body.

Sour horses are scared horses: scared of the crowds or the pain they get when they do the pattern.

But more dangerous than souring is the danger the rider exposes himself to when he uses a whip in competition. Most riders use the whip in the last straight run to the finish line. No rule book permits the use of a whip in front of the girth, so in order to reach the horse well behind, the rider has to turn his head away from the direction he is moving and instead look down or back over his shoulder. The rider is not looking where he is going. Usually he is inadvertently pulling his horse off balance or off course. When the horse hits the wall or stops suddenly, this rider is unprepared and can be thrown far and hard.

If the games are run in heats, horse against horse, it is even more dangerous to use a whip. There have been terrible collisions because riders were so busy whipping that they weren't paying attention to where they were going. There have been broken legs on horses and broken legs on riders because of these accidents.

If your training programme has to include artificial aids for speed and your particular competition allows them, use spurs. Use them as a signal not as an accelerator. Don't dig with them, just press gently. And remember that a horse has to be trained to work with spurs. He has to know what they are there for. Don't just put them on the day of the competition and gouge the animal. Practise getting used to them weeks before the show or rally. Start out by pressing lightly, and keep on pressing them lightly.

If you use one harder than the other, the horse will move to the side rather than forward. Use both spurs too vigorously and the horse may well go straight up, straight backward or kick out instead of moving forward. To gain anything from spurs, the horse and rider have to know what is coming and what is wanted.

But regardless of how you produce and regulate your horse's speed, the bottom line for every games horse is his hooves and what we put on them. Tempting as it might be, do not tell your farrier how to do his job. Choose a farrier you can trust. Explain and discuss your problems, make suggestions and then follow his sage advice. Not only will a qualified farrier have a lot of options at his fingertips, he will also know how they will work under local conditions.

For instance, many games riders are entranced by the idea of studs screwed into their horse's shoes. Scores of books recommend studs for extra security on slippery ground but most of these books are written in countries where rainfall is plentiful and muddy arenas are a fact of life. But 'slippery' means different things in different parts of the world and if it means iron-hard ground baked to a glassy surface, then studs are the last thing you want on your horse's shoes. Under dry, hard conditions those studs will work like ice-skates rather than gym shoes. What dry-ground riders need is a dab or two of borium on the front shoes or even all the way around. Borium is a little more expensive than plain shoes but in some parts of the world, it helps the horse keep his footing. Some people say that borium makes horseshoes last longer, but the main reason *some* riders use it is for their protection and that of their horse. It is not unusual to see even world-class horses fall going around a pole or barrel at speed and any help a farrier can give them in staying upright is worth the expense.

Pony Club riders usually compete in general-purpose English saddles but Western and stock saddle also have their fans. Once again check your organisation, your competition and your rule book. Within those constraints many riders – especially older, heavier ones – choose the lightest edition of their favourite saddle. Individual saddle preferences vary so much but as long as the saddle fits the horse comfortably and is allowed in the rules, the sky is the limit, provided that the stirrups fit your feet and the seat fits yours.

No one can run a games horse successfully and safely unless he can keep his feet in the stirrups. The stirrups are your base and support and if your feet are sliding through them or trapped inside them, your feet and legs will be everywhere, causing you to lose your balance and causing the horse to lose his. Young riders especially always seem to be losing their stirrups. Sometimes it is because they insist on riding with a very long stirrup leather. Often it is because they are using a stirrup that is much too big or too wide. If you find yourself flopping everywhere during a run or lying on your horse's neck, check the size of your stirrup, the length of the leather and how the stirrup is hung on the saddle. If you find that a Western barrel-racing saddle has too much swing

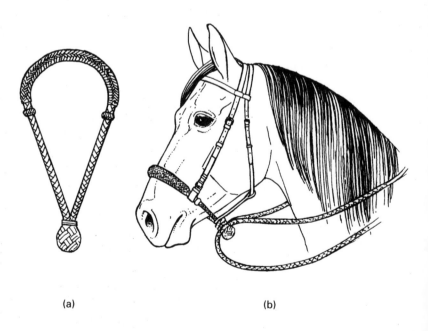

(a)   (b)

A bitless Westen bridle: (a) bosal; (b) the hackamore.

in the stirrup leather for you, try a lightweight pleasure saddle whose stirrups are set a bit forward.

The subject of bits is always a touchy one and as many people err on one side much as on the other. For every rider who uses a bear trap of a bit there is one who under-bits his horse. In open classes where there is a lot of leeway in the type of bit used, we often see small children running the barrels on big horses. Those big horses are going flat out and they are sometimes wearing little aluminium bits and no martingale. The child does the pattern and runs to the arena wall full tilt and then tries to jerk the horse to a stop. It's a wonder that child hasn't had his face broken or been run through the arena fence. When you are running strong and twisting from side to side quickly, a breastplate can snap or a rein can break.

The Pony Club handles this situation by insisting that all tack and equipment be checked by officials before the competition begins. Tent-pegging associations also have a pre-game inspection. All gymkhanas should.

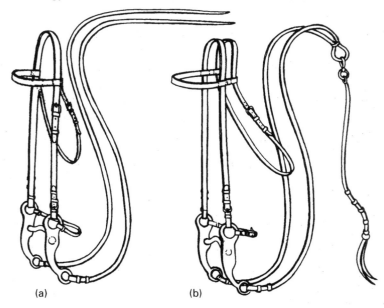

The Western bitted bridle: (a) Texas style, split reins; (b) California style with romal.

7

The Pre-training

Having assembled ourselves, our horse, our position and our equipment, we can now start putting it all together. But whichever level we are training at, whichever event we are preparing for, whichever association rules we ride under, we all follow the same basic training programme and adhere to the same basic principles of warming up before each session. So many people think they can train a games horse or a games rider in two or three days. They get their horse out and, for example, start by trotting him around the poles. Before they know it, they are running *at* the poles. As long as the horse and rider are getting through the pattern without falling down, these riders think that they have a games horse and that they are games riders. He isn't and they aren't.

What they do have is a physically and mentally unbalanced horse who quickly learns that he must run in all directions every time he feels weight in the saddle. The horse, like his rider, is undisciplined, uncomfortable and uncertain of just what it is that he is supposed to do.

To avoid this dangerous situation first make sure that your new prospective games horse is letter-perfect in his basic training. If you have trained him yourself you know his background. If you bought him from someone else you will have asked the previous owner about the horse's history. You have seen him ridden and you have ridden him yourself to find out what he knows and if he needs any correction in his schooling.

But before you actually begin this programme of addition and subtraction, make sure the horse is physically and mentally ready for the lessons. In other words, **every lesson begins with a warm-up**.

When any horse comes out of his stable he is bound to be a little stiff (just as you are when you first get out of bed in the morning). At the same time he is usually mentally ready for anything and eager to take life by the throat. So you want to gradually warm him up and relax his muscles while you cool him down mentally so he will pay attention in class.

Some riders do this by free-schooling their horses in a riding arena or small paddock. Others lunge their horses at the walk and trot because this gives them more control over an animal who might play too hard and injure himself. Yet another warm-up routine is to ride the horse at the walk and trot in big (at least 20 metre) circles with lots of changes of direction.

Whichever your method let the horse trot out at this time and don't antagonise him by fighting him down to a slow jog or forcing him onto the bit. This walking and trotting and bending in big circles on both reins is just exercise, a chance to unwind and stretch before settling down to work.

After walking and trotting, ride your horse around the rail or track, reviewing what you both already know. Walk, trot and canter both ways of the arena. Side-pass and do a little two-track work in both directions. Halt. Back up a few paces.

With some horses and ponies this warm-up takes twenty minutes. Some others will take forty minutes or more on the clock before they are ready to pay attention. After a week or so you will know how much time to allow your particular horse to get ready for serious work. And that is the time you must spend before each lesson.

You cannot skip this pre-training warm-up and you cannot cut it short. If you have only half an hour to ride that day and you know that it takes your horse half an hour to warm up, then cancel the lesson and go for a hack or trail ride instead. Forget about doing anything challenging if you haven't got time to do it right.

A few times in every trainer's life he is going to take a short cut and take that horse in the arena for hard work without warming him up first. That lesson always ends in confusion and frustration at best and a darn good fight at worst. Warming up is a fact of any athlete's life and it cannot be forgotten or cut short if he wants to be successful.

When you feel that your horse is relaxed and paying attention, halt him by the fence and let him catch his breath. Horses cannot be trained and they cannot work unless they have enough air in their lungs. Working a horse until he is breathless is no good; the horse is not trainable at that point and he is ready for injury.

For the people who have broken the legs of games horses, the answer as to how that leg got broken is an easy one. The horse was out of air. He could not get enough oxygen into his system. He tried to run or turn and there was nothing to fuel the engine. At this point he will weaken and take a bad step and possibly break a leg or pull a muscle or strain a tendon.

So pay a lot of attention to warm-ups and rest periods. When you see or feel your games horse panting or breathing heavily, stop and let him get his breath. A games horse will run every time the best he can *if* he is trained and *if* he has enough air. You can practise as much as you like if after you have done a pattern once or twice, you let the horse stand and rest. If you place any value on your horse's life and your own, give your horse sufficient warm-up time and plenty of breaks each time he runs, each time he works.

8

The Barrels

Although rodeo riders love to claim the barrel race as their own, this event really belongs to the whole world of gymkhana. The cloverleaf pattern looks deceptively easy but even if your horse or pony is already proficient at pole-bending, it will still take a month or so of training to prepare him for barrel-racing.

If you haven't done it before, now is the time to study your horse's stride for brushing, over-reaching or any other problems in his way of going. At this point many people go in for specialised shoeing and many barrel-racing riders like to use barrel plates with a rim that is longer on the outside around the toe and shorter on the inside. Other riders prefer a polo plate but, being shorter around the toe, these shoes don't cling as well as the barrel plates do. If your horse travels straight, consider using borium all around (if your conditions require it). If the horse has a tendency to strike himself, ask your farrier about using plain satellite (light) shoes behind. If these are unavailable, ask your farrier what he recommends.

But, remember these are specialised shoes for barrel-racing specialists. Some of them may solve problems you do not have, or they may give you an edge you do not need at your level of competition. Before trying fancy footwork keep in mind the old adage: 'If it ain't broke, don't fix it.' Discuss any and all major shoeing changes with your farrier before committing yourself and your horse.

The same principles used in pole-bending are used in barrel-racing and in fact many trainers like to teach the pole-bending pattern before the barrels. They work on the principle that if the horse can master the more complicated pole-bending then the barrels should come very easily. Others begin with the barrels just because it is less complicated.

First look at the two barrel patterns and choose the one that best suits your horse or pony. Quite a few factors go into deciding which pattern to use and it is important to consider all of them.

If your horse is equally well balanced and supple on both reins then you really don't have much of a problem. You can choose to run either the right- or left-hand barrel first. But if your horse has a decided preference for one lead or bend, then you must weigh up a few factors. There is one lead change in the cloverleaf pattern (halfway between the first and second barrel). If your horse takes his right lead easily then you might want to run to the left barrel first so there will be no hesitation in the lead change between the first and second barrel. Also he will be running two of his three barrels on his most comfortable lead which will give him better balance and time.

On the other hand, if the horse is stiff bending to the right then you might want to make the right-hand barrel your first one, leaving him to run the majority of his barrels to the left. At this point in his training you will have a good idea of your horse's capabilities and can weigh up these factors.

Having planned your pattern, begin walking through it a few times to get your horse used to the new equipment. Then begin working the pattern from a slow sitting trot or jog.

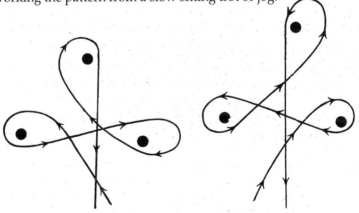

Two variations of the cloverleaf pattern used in barrel racing.

Approach the first barrel wide. That is, pass it about 2½ feet (0.75 m) away from the outside rim. Halt even with the barrel and back the horse a step or two. Trot on to the next barrel. Come in wide and halt. Back up a couple of steps. Trot on to the next barrel, coming in wide. Halt and back up.

Now although you can move up to the slow trot quite early in training for a barrel race, be prepared to stay in the trot for a long time before moving on to the canter. Positioning is very important in the barrel race and any dressage rider will tell you that you have more control over yourself and your horse at the sitting trot than you do at the canter. Both horse and rider have better balance at this gait and it is easier to establish the habit of following the pattern of coming in wide, going away close and halting or hesitating at each barrel.

To explain what is meant by 'going away close' and 'coming in wide' examine the illustration. Let's say that you plan to make your first barrel the left one. This will make your positioning side your left side. Approach the barrel with plenty of room to spare but as you turn the barrel, pass as close to it as you can. At the second barrel, come in wide on the positioning side and go away close to the barrel on 'the running side'. At the third barrel you will also come in wide on the positioning side but as you go away close to the barrel (coming home to the finish line) angle your horse slightly toward the first barrel.

This angling toward the first barrel is an over compensation for the horse's natural tendency to drift toward barrel two. If you do not nip this drifting in the bud very early in his training, the horse will continue to drift toward barrel number two until he is drifting right out of the arena. This will cost you time or the class.

At least two weeks should be spent on teaching your horse and yourself this deceptively easy pattern at the trot. Practise bringing the horse into the barrel wide and coming away close to the barrel. Practise halting and backing at each barrel. This halting and backing will instil in both of you the habit of hesitating or half-halting as you approach a barrel. It is a habit you will come to treasure in the heat of competition when you have to correct position or balance.

Keep the horse between hand and leg at all times. Do not encourage him to lean into or 'bank' his turns. When he crosses from barrel one to barrel two, always ride a straight line so that he will be in the habit of keeping himself straight and upright when you come to ask for the flying lead change there.

Leaning into turns is a great temptation to barrel-racers who do a lot of bicycle and motorbike riding. It seems like the natural way to travel when going around a corner at speed. But the more you lean into your turns the better your chances are of getting 'rimmed' and the better your horse's chances are of falling down. ('Rimmed' is the single most excrutiating pain you can achieve on a horse. It happens when you pass a barrel so closely that your shin is barked on the metal rim. It is a pain beyond swearing and crying. It is the kind of pain that makes you feel sick. Many riders wrap their legs with track bandages or wear soccer leg guards under their jeans and jodhpurs to avoid being rimmed.)

At the walk, the trot and the canter, you are bending the horse around your inside leg as you turn the barrel. To do this, push with your outside leg behind the girth. If you choose to ride one-handed, hold the saddle horn or pommel with your free hand.

It is imperative to turn the barrel in an upright and balanced position. It saves time and knees.

When turning your barrel, come in wide and leave close to the barrel on a straight line.

This will pull you down in the saddle and hold you steady. The steadier you are in your position the faster you can sense when your horse is slipping out of the correct position and the faster you can correct him. This hold on the horn, pommel or breast-plate strap will also hold you in place as the turns become faster and sharper. As your position becomes stronger and a habit you can take for granted, your mind will be free to concentrate on the instant decisions you will have to make when riding in competition. Remember that although we want to train a pattern horse, we never want to become pattern riders. There are too many variables in competition to go to sleep at the wheel.

Establishing an upright position for both horse and rider requires a lot of concentration, a lot of repetition and a lot of muttering, 'Come in wide, go away close and keep both of us upright and straight.' But it is worth it.

Why is straightness so important? Because a straight horse is balanced and a balanced horse is comfortable and unrestricted. He has no need to develop bad habits. He is able to change leads easily on command. He won't resist your requests. After all, bad habits are formed when a horse is thrown off balance and has to twist his body to save himself or to get out of an uncomfortable position.

To avoid putting your horse in an uncomfortable position you come in wide and continue far enough past the barrel so the horse will have enough room to manoeuvre, enough room to avoid hitting the barrel or falling off balance. By giving the horse enough room to operate, you avoid forcing him to lean in and throw his weight too much to the inside.

(In actual competition you can start skimming a little off your wide approach. You may not have to go out quite as wide as you did in the early days because now the horse is fitter and able to work a smaller turn with ease. But after the competition, take him home and practise the pattern as you did in the beginning of his training so he can retain his good habits.)

What happens when you don't reinforce these good habits? The horse may well start cheating the barrel. He may try to cut his corner too sharply and then be forced to throw his weight to the inside instead of remaining upright and in balance. We often see it, and the rider can feel it because his weight will be thrown onto his own inside leg. The horse's and the rider's weight are then thrown onto the horse's inside legs and because this weight is not distributed evenly, there is a chance that the horse will slip and fall.

Another possibility is that the horse will be forced to turn so close to the barrel that he or the rider will hit the barrel. In many competitions if the horse or rider knocks the barrel over, that entry will be disqualified.

Once the horse starts turning too closely or cheating the barrel, the cure is often worse than the original problem. The rider tries to pull the horse's head away from the barrel to keep the horse from leaning in. When the rider releases that pull to allow the horse to turn the barrel, the horse's head swings hard to the inside and the hindquarters swing hard to the outside of the turn. The horse, off balance and in pain, stumbles and slows down, losing time and sometimes his rider.

We also see this effect when riders move up to the canter. Instead of holding their horse upright and straight for the flying lead change between the first and second barrel, some riders try to throw their horse into a lead change by changing the bend sharply and without warning. They feel that a sudden fierce change of direction will accomplish everything. It accomplishes what throwing your horse off balance always accomplishes. . .

The straight approach to the barrels, both by the path taken and by keeping the horse upright and straight, is the simplest part of training and it is where most pole and barrel horses are ruined. As long as you progress gradually through walk, trot, canter and run in a straight and upright fashion, each step will follow the other in a logical and comfortable progression.

9

Pole-bending

Now that you have barrel-racing and a number of novelty games under control you may want to stop right here. Magnolia Missile won over $300,000 as a barrel-racer and his owner Lynn McKenzie was absolutely thrilled. Sharon Camarillo has made a whole career out of training and competing barrel-racers. Some associations give national championships in the flag race alone, and like these winners you may feel that specialisation is the way to go. However, if you and your horse have a flair for flying changes and a desire to expand your mounted games repertoire, why not consider pole-bending?

Pole-bending is the *lingua franca* of mounted games. We find this slalom pattern in Pony Club, rodeo, open games classes and breed shows. When we hear that there are mounted games on the programme we can be sure that one of them will be pole-bending because of its popularity and universal appeal.

Terry Thompson won his first US Appaloosa World Championship when he was nineteen years old and is now considered one of the masters of pole-bending. Examine the two most popular pole-bending patterns on page 68 and listen to what Terry has to say about conquering them:

'The first steps in training for this event are taken at the walk. Your horse is warmed up and ready to do a flat-footed walk calmly. If he isn't, go back to your warm-up routine until he is ready.

'Unlike a dressage horse, we want a pole-bender to know his pattern. So I start walking the horse through the poles to give him an idea of where he is supposed to go. I walk him to the first pole and then two-track or leg yield him between that and the second pole. I come in wide,

When trotting your horse through the poles, take the reins in both hands to encourage correct balance in yourself and your horse.

not getting too close to the pole I'm passing. I don't want to give my horse any ideas about coming too close to the pole. I want him calm and under control. So just at the walk I two-track between poles 1 and 2 and then I let him walk forward and then two-track back the other way between 2 and 3.

'I'm not trying to hold this horse in any special position because he doesn't really know what he is doing at this point. I just want him to get the idea and the basic motion of passing between the poles. I just keep working back and forth between the poles (without stopping to correct him) until he gets the idea on his own. I'll do this pattern five or six times and then I'll come back to an imaginary starting line and halt to rest him.

'I do this perhaps four times and then I take him to the rail of the arena and walk, trot and canter him both ways of the arena. Or I take him out on the trails or work cattle. . . anything completely different.

'The important thing is that I've warmed him up calmly and I've worked him calmly. He has reviewed his old lessons before he has been asked to learn something new and he repeated his old lessons before he

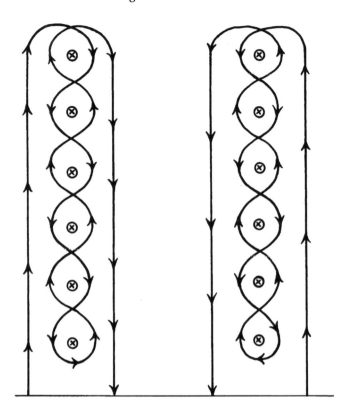

Variations on the pole-bending pattern often found in open, full width competition.

has been put out to play. He has gotten exercised but he hasn't gotten excited, doing a lot of prancing and dancing in one spot. After a week of this, the horse is becoming familiar with the pattern and with the routine.

'When my horse is side-passing/two-tracking through the poles easily and lightly, moving away from my leg and not being hauled across by the mouth, only then do we move up to the trot.

'At the trot it is the same motion and the same routine. I like to use a bosal and tie-down, his saddle and breastplate with sheepskin covers and his splint boots. Other riders may prefer a snaffle bridle and a martingale.

'At this slow trot we'll again be doing the two-tracking motion between the poles. When we trot to the poles we stay 12–15 feet [3.6–4.5 m] away from them. Now I am introducing him to pattern 2 [page 68]. I trot until the first pole is even with my horse's hip or the back part of the saddle. At this point I say, 'Whoa, stop him and back him a few paces. I might do this several times just to get him used to the idea of stopping and also to see how much 'whoa' this horse has in him. If the horse does not stop readily, this is the time to begin teaching him to do so.

'*I never introduce a horse to run until I have introduced him to stop.* If a horse has never learned to slow down and stop on command, his games career is beat, beat, beat, whip, whip, whip and run into a wall to stop. His rider has little control over this horse's position and none over his speed.

'I want to teach every horse that stopping (and resting) are the rewards for doing his job right. Stopping or pausing also introduce him to calmness and paying attention to his rider. But it is no good working on 'stop' when the horse is fresh out of the stable and it is a cold, windy day. The horse has to have something to rest *from* and this is another reason we want to work our horses in well before doing the specialised training. You can avoid a lot of problems and fights if you put your horse

At first, side-passing your horse through the poles will get some over-reaction in your horse's head and neck position. With practice, his position will become more relaxed and balanced.

When you move up to canter, remember to sit upright and maintain your own balence, especially when rounding your final pole. Keep your reins in both hands to correct balance.

in a position where he wants to do your bidding. Wait until he is looking for a rest, then ask for a halt. It makes life a lot easier for both of you.

'After halting and back, I walk the horse around the end pole and start his two-tracking movement through the pattern. I halt at each pole and then two-track through it. When I get to the end pole I trot the horse a little way past it (until the pole is behind the saddle and the horse is about 10 feet [3 m] away from the pole). I stop, back up and then trot the horse around the pole.

'At this point we may walk back to the starting line or we may trot back to it. I may just let him sit and rest at the final pole. I don't need to take him back at speed each time.

'I repeat this exercise of trotting and halting and two-tracking four or five times. This makes the horse familiar with the pattern quickly and it gives him the idea of 'halt and listen.' But even so it will take the average horse at least a month of trot and extended trot before he is ready to

70

move up to the slow canter.

'I say 'canter' but it is often a case of trot sometimes and canter some-times. For instance, if we are doing the pattern from right to left, I canter down on the left lead because I want to instil the habit of his taking the left lead when I put my right leg on him. I push him a little beyond the end pole and then I stop and let him rest. Then I canter him around the end pole so he bends around it correctly and in balance.

'At the canter the side-pass/two-track motion becomes a straight and balanced and upright flying lead change. He has the idea of side move-ment at walk and trot and when executed at the canter, it becomes a lead change.

'In pole-bending the first end pole is crucial. It is important to keep the horse upright at all times. If he starts leaning into poles, banking his turns, he will soon start dropping his shoulder. This causes him to throw his hindquarters out and his body will be thrown off balance.

'If you are having trouble hitting the end pole, chances are you are let-ting the horse lean into his turns. You are not pushing the horse far enough past the end pole before turning him. You are turning the horse too soon.

'Another fault is pulling the reins too hard and that also can throw the horse onto his inside shoulder which forces him to throw his hip away from the pole. This sling-shot action is painful for the horse and it makes it harder for him to keep his balance.

'No one wants his horse to lean in and suck into that pole. What we want is a horse listening to us when we check him and we want him pro-ducing that correct sweeping two-track motion at the canter. We want the horse moving away from leg pressure. We want to be able to push him over an inch or clear to the wall if we need to.

'How do we achieve all this?

'In pole-bending the games rider's instant decisions are very impor-tant and very apparent. These adjustments are a case of when to release the horse into his turns and the first and most important turn is the one off the starting line. You must get the horse off that line in the correct position, on the correct lead and on the bit.

'Releasing consists of just moving your hands slightly forward or opening your fingers and letting out the impulsion that your seat and legs have created.

'Checking is harder. It isn't a full stop, a true halt. It is an instant's pause almost in mid-air. It is what the dressage riders call a half-halt. To do it push with your seat and legs and hold with your hands at the instant the horse is bringing his legs under him.

'With that in mind, try a practice run.

'At the starting line or just behind it hold the horse with your right hand over and your left hand against his neck. The horse is upright and when you release him he will fall on to the other lead. It is on the first turn that we make or break our pole-bending run.

'Release the horse onto the correct lead. You have turned around the pole and so have gotten him to the starting point. You have decided when to release him so he can turn the pole. Now check him and decide when to release him on the right side so he can start his sweep to the second pole.

'If you have released the horse too soon, he will hit the pole. As you turn the end pole approach it wide, moving away from it. Then go back close making the decision when to release the horse into his next lead change. If he hits the pole with his shoulder, you have made the mistake. If he hits it with the tail, he has made the mistake.

'I do these cantering exercises in a series so that when I do the final straight trip to the finish line, the horse is worked up a little bit. He is excited and I give him the idea of motion at the canter. I take him to the finish line at the canter, stop him and let him stand and relax. I always do the pattern in the same direction because I want my horse to know his pattern cold.

'This halting and resting is also very important. It encourages the horse to keep calm and it makes sure that he has plenty of air. Often you see a games horse throwing his head after a run. He may be breathless and trying to catch his breath. When we run fast and get out of breath, we can stop but the horse is not allowed to stop. He is often whipped and spurred to keep going and when he does (under these conditions) he is in a dangerous situation.

'After a while the trainer, like any other teacher, has to give his student a test to find out how much he has learned. I am going to ask my horse for speed – not a dead run – but something faster than a canter. I am not going to halt him but just take him through the whole pattern just as I would in competition. By now the horse should have enough check in him so that if I just say 'Whoa' and feel the reins, he should pause or halt.

'At this point I can tell if my horse has any real ability. If he has it, the test should be easy for him, though there may be a few rough spots. Maybe he won't have his hindquarters under him at the end pole (in which case, use your outside leg on him to bring his hindquarters in and under him).

'I think it is very important to test your horse every once in awhile. Remember, we train a horse through his mistakes and if you never let him go, never put him on his own so he can make a mistake, then we cannot help him to improve. Professional trainers in particular are prone to helping their horses too much. These riders hold their horse by the reins and keep the horse under such control that the horse cannot learn to maintain his balance on his own.

'(An equivalent of this is the event or show jumping rider who always schools his horse over jumps in an arena or goes very carefully over the odd cross-country jump. He never takes his horse hunting to give him a chance to find a leg or gain some independence. When the time comes to do a cross-country course at speed the horse cannot think for himself. If he gets in trouble show jumping the horse has no ability to save himself. He is totally dependent on his rider and even then may not be able to take correction at speed.)

'Right here, after you have asked your pole-bending horse for speed once or twice, is a good time to give that horse a little break in his schooling. For a week or two I'll just hack the horse or do stock work. I let him forget about gymkhana school and relax. All this time the horse has been ridden in a bosal or light snaffle. If there comes a time when the bosal is not enough to hold your horse then it has outlived its usefulness and you should go to a mild snaffle bit for more control.

'After this break we are ready to begin the second phase of our training. Now we begin asking for more speed and it is very important that our horse is fully trained and knows his pattern. At this point we can let him go to see what we both have accomplished. If he makes a mistake at speed, we can correct him. Direct him. Correct him. But do not punish him for an error. Spurring and whipping don't help and they especially don't help a games horse. The only thing physical punishment will do is upset him.

Working a games horse at speed and putting him on his own with a minimum of direction teaches him to get himself out of trouble. If he cannot do the pattern himself (or get out of trouble) I can correct him on the spot or pick him up and move him into the correct position. If he is about to hit a pole, I can collect him with the reins and move him over with my leg. If he has had the experience of being corrected or adjusted at home, I can make a correction at a show and it won't shatter him.

'This correction and refining of technique is an everyday process and it is a chore. Sometimes it means changing or adjusting his tack a little. Maybe he needs a dropped noseband; maybe he needs a hackamore. Because my horse is moving faster with more impulsion I am going to have to have additional control over him that a different bit or noseband can give me.

'During this third month I am letting both of us get used to this new equipment. I am learning how much hold to take of the reins and how hard the horse will run into his tie-down or martingale so I will know how to set it. I will continue to use splint boots on the front legs and possibly bell boots as well. The horse may hit himself in the back legs once or twice but unless there is something physically wrong with him, he will soon learn to handle his hindquarters at speed. If he really has a problem over-reaching I'll put bell boots on the front feet but I hate doing it. I feel that bell boots get in a sprinter's way, like putting gum boots on a track star.'

So now we have realised more than ever how important control and attention to detail – both in equipment and in training – are to a successful mounted games horse. When you consider the movements demanded of him at speed and the control the rider must have in order to help his horse perform theses movements, we realise how remarkable these horses and riders are.

10

Twenty Top Games

By now it has occurred to you that the type of games you meet at gymkhanas and horse shows (as opposed to those played at camps and riding schools) come in three main styles. There is the RIDE THE PATTERN AS FAST AS YOU CAN type, like keyhole race, barrel race and pole-bending. There is the RIDE, DO SOMETHING, AND RIDE BACK variety, like apple-bobbing, musical sacks and boot race. And finally, there is the RIDE WHILE YOU ARE DOING SOMETHING style, like flag race, egg-and-spoon and water race. Within these three loose classifications is a mass of variations on the fun and excitement theme. To get you running around in circles as well as in straight lines, here are twenty games you might like to try. If they are not described exactly the way you play them, it is because they have been collected from the United Kingdom, Australia, New Zealand, Canada and the United States, and like horsemen, they vary a little from place to place but are always a lot of fun.

Ride and Lead

Ride down to the marker, dismount and lead back. Depending on the expertise of the riders, you may want to stipulate that contestants walk down as fast as they can, or trot, canter, or even flat gallop.

Apple-Bobbing

Wherever you have apples, this event is a classic. For each contestant, supply a bucket or pan with an interesting amount of water and an apple. The riders line up on the starting line and, at the signal, get down to their buckets as fast as they can. They dismount and, holding their pony, remove the apple from the bucket without using their hands. For the less expert you may want to supply horse holders while the riders are capturing the apples. In some events the riders must ride back across the finish line (having spat out the apple before mounting). In others the game is over as soon as a rider emerges from the bucket with an apple in his teeth.

Barrel Racing

The patterns and training for the class have been dealt with in Chapter 8. For some riders barrel racing is just one of a series of games. For others it is a whole career in itself. Going off course or tipping over a barrel may result in elimination or time penalties. Hitting a barrel with your shins or knees always results in agony.

Pole-Bending

Like barrel racing, pole-bending rates a chapter to itself (see Chapter 9). Although the pattern may vary from country to coun-

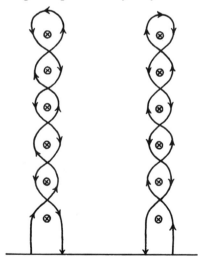

Two variations on the pole-bending pattern used in Pony Club competition.

try or association to association, the rules remain the same. Going off course or hitting a pole are both penalised. Sometimes this means elimination, sometimes time penalties are added to the rider's score.

Egg and Spoon

Each rider is issued with a large spoon and an egg to carry in it; reins in one hand, spoon in the other. Until the class begins, riders hold their egg in place with their thumb but at the command 'Thumbs up!', it is balance alone that keeps the egg in the spoon. At this point the class is in the hands of the judge who can call for walk, trot, canter, reverse and may even set up a few low jumps. As the eggs fall so are the riders eliminated until the winner stands alone in the arena with his egg still in his spoon.

A variation on this has the rider ride around a marker, return to the centre line, pick up an egg and spoon and lead the pony to the finish line without touching the egg with his hand at any time.

Boot Race

This event enjoys great popularity at university horse shows in North America where the riders are experienced and seemingly immune to embarrassment. Riders line up on the starting line and remove one or both boots. The footgear is collected and placed in pairs at the end of the arena. At a signal the riders race to the boots, dismount, put them on and ride for the finish line.

Ribbon Race

Each pair of riders is given a long streamer of crepe paper, a rider holding each end. At the signal the twosome rides down to the end of the arena, around a marker and back across the finish line without breaking the fragile streamer.

Trotting Race

A marker is placed or a line drawn at the far end of the arena. The riders trot up to and around the marker or cross the line and trot back. If the pony breaks gait the rider is either eliminated or must circle before continuing (depending on the rules of the particular show).

Rescue Race

Each horse and rider team has an unmounted rider waiting at the far end of the arena. At the signal the horse and rider race down to the end of the arena, pick up the second rider behind and the riders ride double back to the finish line. In the interests of safety it is suggested that individual runs are timed.

Keyhole Race

A keyhole shape is drawn on the ground with chalk, lime or saw-dust. Horse and rider stand at the starting line and at the signal, canter down into the keyhole and without stepping outside the line, turn around and gallop back across the line. (See diagram).

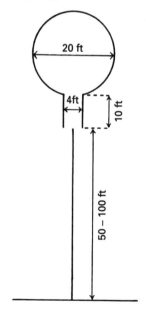

Keyhole pattern.

Unsaddling Race

Each contestant is stationed on the starting line, in his particular lane. At the opposite end of the arena is a marker or line. The riders gallop to the marker or across the line, halt, dismount, run up their stirrups (if using a hunt saddle) and remove the saddle. The riders remount their horses bareback and ride back across the starting/finish line. Falls or failure to run up English saddle stirrups result in elimination.

Musical Sacks

A number of feed sacks (one less than the number of entries) are placed in the centre of the arena. The riders follow each other around the edge of arena while music plays. When the music stops, the riders dismount and run with their ponies to a sack in the centre. Anyone not standing on a sack is eliminated. A feed sack (or mat) is removed at each round so there is always one less than the number of riders. The game continues until only one rider is left. Anyone riding (instead of dismounting and leading) is eliminated.

Sack Race

At the end of the arena is a marker or line. A large hessian sack is provided for each contestant. From this point on, sack races come in a variety of forms. Some feature the rider going down to the end at speed, turning around, riding to the centre line, dismounting, climbing into his sack and leading his pony back to the finish line from within the sack. Others put their entries in their sacks on the starting line and riders begin shuffling and jumping towards the far line while leading their ponies. Some allow the rider to hold the sack in his free hand. Others insist that the sack must be over the knees when he crosses the finish line. The simpler the game, the more refinements are possible.

Simon Says

This is a terrific equaliser for the less than brilliant athlete - equine or human. Riders line up. circle, or arrange themselves around the arena in clear view of the judge. The judge then calls out random commands, such as 'Stand in your stirrups!' or 'Flying dismount!'. The only commands that must be obeyed are those that are introduced by the words 'Simon Says'. Anyone obeying a 'false' command, or failing to obey a 'true' one is eliminated or penalised.

Command

In some breed associations this class has been elevated to an art form. The judge gives commands while the riders circle him on the edge of the arena. 'Walk', 'Trot', 'Canter', 'Back up', 'Reverse' and 'Halt' are the common commands and they must be obeyed instantly. A wrong lead or the movement of a single foot when halt has been called result in elimination. Breaking gait or taking too long to obey a command culls most of the riders but sometimes a real battle of wills and wits results in commands like 'Reverse at the canter with a flying change of lead', to break a tie! When commanded to 'Back up', the riders must continue backing their horses (sometimes a complete circuit of the arena) until a new command is given.

Saddle-up Race

Each contestant unsaddles his pony and puts his saddle on the line at the far end of the arena. He returns to the starting line and remounts. At the signal he rides down to his saddle, dismounts, saddles his pony, mounts and returns to the starting line. In some games the rider must have both feet in the stirrups and all the girth buckles must be correctly and securely fastened or the rider is eliminated.

Stake Race

A variation on pole-bending, a stake race is always run in heats, horse against horse. The losing horse is eliminated. Knocking down a stake, turning the wrong way, or a rider touching a stake with his hand will result in elimination unless the other rider makes a similar mistake. In that case the race is re-run. (See diagram.)

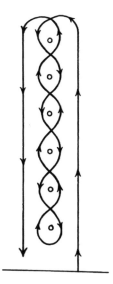

Stake race pattern.

Walk, Trot and Canter

At the far end of the arena is the ubiquitous marker or cone. Each rider walks to the marker, turns and trots to the starting line and then gallops to the marker and back to the finish line. If the pony breaks to a slower pace there is no penalty but if he breaks to a faster gait than the one indicated, then he must circle before continuing.

Sit-a-Buck

In prosperous times a dollar bill or pound note is put under each rider's bottom or under his thigh (with most of the paper exposed). More thrifty shows may want to use a strip of paper. All riders are bareback. The class is then called like any other: walk, trot, canter, reverse, etc. As each rider's paper is lost, that rider is eliminated until only one remains with his paper still in place.

Obstacle Race

Select three or four races and combine them in a single mind-boggling event!

11

Pony Club in Particular

Although tent-pegging, barrel-racing and pole-bending are hotly contested all over the world, when horsemen think of children and mounted games they immediately think of the Pony Club Mounted Games Championships, a team event known to Pony Club members everywhere as the Prince Philip Cup Games. The lead-up to the finals (at the Horse of the Year Show in London) are held all over the United Kingdom during the spring and summer holidays and, for Pony Club members of at least one year's standing and under fifteen of age, these lead-up competitions and training sessions are what mounted games are all about.

For those overseas members of the Pony Club who cannot be in England now that spring is here, Pony Clubs in Canada, New Zealand and Australia have their own Prince Philip Cup Games and those in the United States Pony Club have the Mounted Games of the United States. Although the top competitions are limited to Pony Club members of tender years, most Pony Clubs allow adult and associate members to participate in local competitions and training sessions. So for young and not so young, membership of the Pony Club is an excellent way to gain exposure to the full range of mounted games and experienced coaching in how to play them.

Like most organised competitions for children, Pony Club mounted games abound in rules and regulations designed to protect the safety of both child and pony and to make sure that competitive zeal is kept under control. For instance no pony over 14.2 hh (+ 2 inches (50 mm) for shoes) nor any pony under four years of age may compete in the Prince Philip Cup Games. No child who weighs more than 53 kg (in riding kit) may ride a pony 12.2 hh or under. Martingales and nosebands may be used but ponies aiming at UK Pony Club competition must be ridden in a plain, smooth snaffle bit – either bar type or with a single centre joint.

(The same pony may hack in a double bridle, jump in a Kimblewick or hunt in a Pelham, but when he is running flat out with a group of like-minded ponies at the Prince Philip Games his rider must be able to control him in a snaffle. If some gymkhana riders question the logic of *this* rule, they universally applaud the Pony Club stand on whips and spurs. Neither is allowed.)

What *is* allowed, in fact what is insisted upon, is safe, appropriate riding gear and attire. If the mandatory light-coloured jodhpurs, jodhpur boots, long-sleeved white shirt, black or blue helmet (conforming to appropriate national standards) all seem a little regimented, there are many good reasons for it. This attire has stood the test of time as the most comfortable, safe and efficient clothing you can wear when playing a huge variety of mounted games.

In addition the Pony Club has many strong ties to the military and they are the first to recognise that a common uniform builds *espirit de corps* in team members and keeps everyone on the same level (sartorially speaking). When everyone wears identical riding kits, no one child can be made to feel superior or inferior by the cut or quality of his coat.

Just as helmets must be worn with a chin strap so all tack must be in good condition and fastened down properly. This tack must also be clean and in good repair. Games riders all over the world realise that their lives depend on sound supple tack and strong stitching. Every rider, no matter what his association or rule book, recommends that equipment be cleaned and checked constantly.

But though every group recommends this inspection, the Pony Club insists on it. And to make sure there are no lapses in this attention to detail, official Pony Club gymkhanas as well as rallies hold an inspection of each rider and mount before the games begin. If there is loose stitching or rotten leather or anything else that might endanger life and limb, that child and pony must rectify the situation or not participate that day. If this seems hard, so is the ground when it is hit at speed.

When each participant has passed inspection (and in competition no one can change his approved equipment after passing inspection) the games begin. One look at the Pony Club's *Gymkhanas and Rally Games* will set any rider aquiver with anticipation. Pony Club offers a veritable cornucopia of contests. They range from leading-rein classes to jumping to apple-bobbing, in short just about anything a child and pony can do together. If some games bore (or terrify) a rider, rest assured that there are masses more that will appeal.

Although any of the games in the Pony Club's *Gymkhanas and Rally Games* can be used at Pony Club gymkhanas and rallies, in the interest of convenience and sanity, the six games, plus a warm-up race and a tie-breaker which will be used at official area competitions for the Prince Philip Cup, are announced every year in November. Along with these come ten games (plus tie-breaker) which will be used for the Zone Finals. The games for the Area level of the Prince Philip Cup are not only announced but also demonstrated at a Mounted Games Study Day at the British Equestrian Centre at Stoneleigh in Warwickshire.

Other countries handle this in different ways and any Pony Club members aiming for their particular national mounted games titles should ask their instructors about the relevant details. Another reason to contact your local and national Pony Club is that not all Pony Club rules are universal. Some areas and some nations waive or adjust rules to fit their particular conditions. For instance, there are parts of the world where riders would be hard-pressed to find a pony of the right size and shape but where horses are more easily had. In some parts of the world Pony Club members compete in stock saddles or Western gear if that is their preference.

So, like a lot of good things, the appeal of Pony Club mounted games is universal but each part of the world may put its own individual stamp on them. The best way to gain the maximum amount of enjoyment out of your entry into this phase of competition is to invest in a good mount and a current rule book for your particular area. These rule books not only tell you how to play the games but also how to organise, judge and win them too.

12

Tent-pegging

We have seen how Pony Club games make a speciality of versatility. Riders leap on and off their ponies, run beside them and deal with stuffed socks, empty bottles, floating apples and a myriad other props and skills. Pole-bending, barrel-racing, keyhole race and straight barrels make a party piece out of speed and action. These riders never leave their saddles and that is no easy trick when your horse's speciality is flying lead changes, 360° turns and/or instant stops. These mounted games bring everyone in the audience to his feet, cheering and clapping. Tent-pegging, however, brings the heart to your throat.

Wherever the British Army trod two-hundred-plus years ago, there you will find keen tent-peggers today. Zimbabwe, Australia, Canada, the Middle East, South Africa and India all have teams of adult riders, and some even have events for riders under fifteen years of age. These tent-pegging events and competitions started off as exercises for the mounted troops, to test their proficiency with lance or sword. A rifleman would go to the range to test his marksmanship. A trooper would do tent-pegging to prove his expertise. Like a lot of things associated with the cavalry, tent-pegging was such a good idea that teams were formed to continue these mounted games even after the military mechanised.

To find out about your local competitions and competitors, write to your national equestrian body who will send you the appropriate names, addresses and rules. Most important, they will put you in touch with experienced coaches who can introduce you safely to the real image of war without its guilt: tent-pegging.

What you will learn will sound very much like the following (with a few local variations).

Although tent-pegging can be done alone, in pairs or in threes, a tent-pegging team is usually made up of four riders. At the judge's signal they ride into the arena, line up and, one after another, gallop down a line of wooden pegs (30cm/1ft high and 7.5cm/3 inches wide and pounded into the ground to a depth of 2.5cm/1 inch). Each rider picks up a peg on the end of his lance or sword and gallops away with it. The pegs are put in the ground either 1.5m (56 inches) apart in a single file or 2.5m (8 feet) apart if the riders are coming four abreast. A round consists of at least one run in single file followed by a run four abreast, and a competitive event has at least three rounds.

Scoring is done by trained, official and graded judges and many calculations go into their decisions. A **carry** is worth 6 points and the peg must be removed from the ground and carried at least 20m (64 feet) on the end of the lance or sword. A **draw** removes the peg but carries it less than 20m (64 feet) and is worth 4 points. A **strike** earns 2 points and indicates that the peg has been hit with the sword or lance but not removed from the ground.

The pegs must be struck on the face of the peg with the point of the weapon and the points involved are razor-sharp and more than adequate for the task.

Engaging the peg in tent-pegging. Reach down, not out.

Upon engaging the peg, let the lance follow through before returning it to the 'present' position.

Whilst this may seem complicated enough there is even more to tent-pegging than just removing the peg and carrying it away.

For starters: up to 8 bonus points (in addition to the pegging points) can be earned in each round for **drill, pace**, and **style**. The phase of the judging starts at the beginning salute and finishes after the pegs are removed following the four abreast run. The **pace** desired is a full gallop, which must be attained at marker A and maintained until marker D. A slow, thoughtful pace earns low points. Each rider must maintain his numerical position in single file or four abreast; there should be no passing or working out of order. Each rider must take his own peg – not his neighbour's. Correct spacing between riders must be maintained at all times.

There is a different **drill** for each weapon used. Many riders make their own lances out of aluminium tubing, and no matter what that rider's height his lance cannot be shorter than 2.5m (8 feet) nor longer than 2.75m (nearly 9 feet). Swords can also be homemade but every tent-pegger dreams of a real cavalry light horse weapon and antique arms shops of the world are scoured for them.

Tent-pegging horses must be at least 14.2 hh with an allowance of 16mm (almost ¾ inch) for shoes, and each horse must wear a breast-plate. Each tent-pegging weapon must have a protective cover over the point (when not in use), and each rider must wear a crash helmet meeting the standards of the relevant governing body.

Once you have assembled your kit, find a good instructor to tell you what to do with it. Galloping a horse flat out towards an unsuspecting wooden peg with a killing blade in your hand is not something to be learned by yourself with a book in one hand. Your coach will keep you, your horse and you team-mates safe and effective and he is worth keeping once you find him (or her).

LANCE DRILL   The lance is carried in a uniform position at the carry or at the trail when approaching the B marker flag. At this

The 'present' position of the lance in tent-pegging. Try to keep the lance perpendicular.

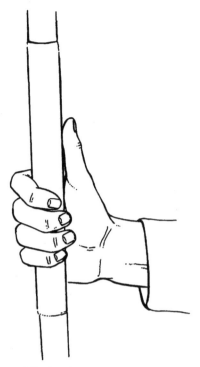

The correct way to present the lance.

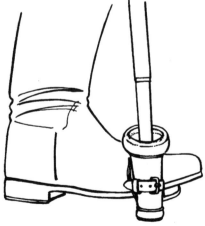

A tent-pegger's cup for a lance in transit.

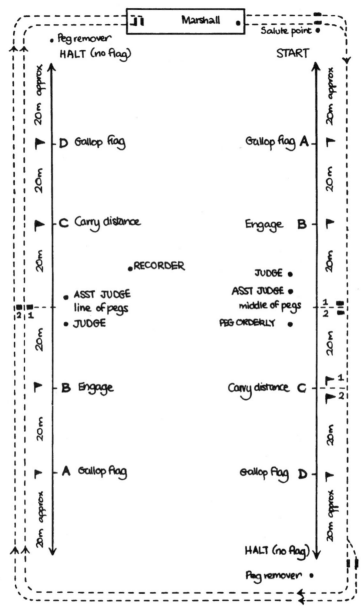

Layout of tent-pegging course for pairs.

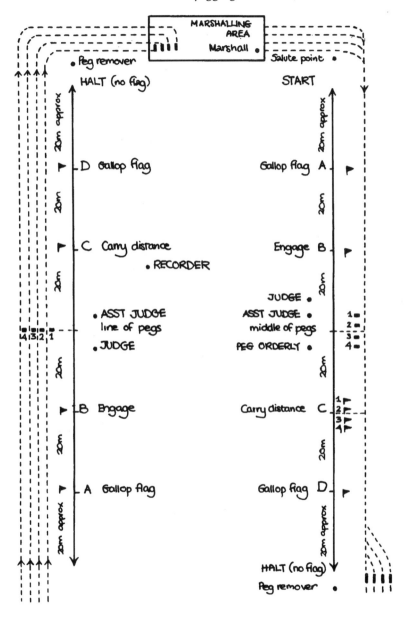

Layout of tent-pegging course for teams of four.

marker the rider presents the lance by thrusting it forward in a vertical position about halfway along the horse's neck. An instant later he lowers the lance to engage his peg. After picking up the peg, he returns the lance through the 'present' position to the carry or trail position. This whole run should take about five seconds.

SWORD DRILL   When approaching the peg in either single file or four abreast, carry the sword at the slope. At marker flag A bring the sword into the straight arm engage (edge outwards!). At B turn the sword edge down – pause slightly – and lower the point to engage the peg. Then carry the sword through to the rear above the level of the right shoulder. After another instant's pause, return the sword to the front position with an underhand sweep and a straight arm. Pause again slightly and resume the slope position.

Obviously, this is not the sort of thing you can practise without professional help. Tent-pegging associations are enthusiastic and generous with their coaches, and schools can be set up for novice horses and riders. These authorities can teach you weapon drill and help to train your horse, as well as advising you how to earn the 20 points for 'Best Turned-out Team or Section'.

They can also introduce you to additional events like 'Rings and Pegs', 'Lemons and Pegs' and the heart-stopping 'Skill at Arms'. Although the general competition is called tent-pegging, horses and riders are not confined to dealing with blocks of wood. In **Rings and Pegs**, the rider must not only pick up his peg, but he must also engage both rings. Rings are a little over 6mm (¼ inch) in diameter and they hang from two gallows with a T-bar about 2.75m (9 feet) off the ground. The rider gallops in, raises his lance to engage one ring after the other (threading them on his lance) and then lowers the lance to pick up the peg as well.

Lemons and Pegs is the sword version of the above, but instead of rings suspended from the T-bar we have real lemons hanging from a string. The rider goes down the line at the gallop and presents his sword. When he reaches the B marker he places his sword horizontally on his shoulder at the base of his neck (blade edge to the rear). He cuts the first lemon in two from right to left, and cuts the second lemon from left to right. Then he lowers his sword to engage the peg and gallops on with the normal sword recover, leaving two halves of lemon behind him.

But if these events are thrilling for everyone, the real party-piece for tent-peggers is the **Skill at Arms**. In this class the rider is armed with a lance, a sword and a steel-pointed cap pistol. Instead of the straight run of previous events, this course involves a Z-shaped run. Even reading a description of 'Skill at Arms' requires a good deal of attention so we will quote from the Australian Tent-pegging Association Rule Book:

'1st leg – shall comprise 2 jumps, 70cms [2 feet 3 inches] high, 2.5m [8 feet] wide and 20m [64 feet)] apart. A balloon holder (1.5 m[56 inches] high) to be placed on right of first jump, another balloon holder on the left of second jump, with a third balloon holder on the right, 20m [64 feet] from 2nd jump (0.5m [1 foot 6 inches] high and in line with the first balloon). The second jump is to be in a central position on the first leg. A barrel or bucket (approx. 20 litre [4 gallon], plastic) is to be placed at the end of first leg, approximately 1.2m [3 feet 9 inches] above ground level.

'2nd Leg – comprises 2 'Turks' heads' on stands (approx. 2m [6ft 6 inches] high with 10cm [4 inch] 'neck' made of 1.5cm [½inch] dowel). The stands to be 15m [48 feet], with the second stand 1.5m [56 inches] to the left of the line of the first stand and dummy. The dummy is to be suspended from a gallows which will swivel away from the rider on impact and located 20m [64 feet] from the second 'Turk's head'. The heart of the dummy is to be 8cm [3 inches] in diameter and 1.6m [5 feet] above ground level.'

What do you with all these items is this:

The rider leaves the starting position armed with a cap pistol to be drawn at least 40m [128 feet] before the first jump (with the pistol's barrel perpendicular). Using one jab per balloon, shoot each balloon as you go over the jump. One refusal is allowed at the first jump only.

On the second leg, draw your sword and, just like in 'Lemons and Pegs' cut through the 'neck' with a forward sweep on the first head and a return sweep on the second. Then, with a straight arm, engage the heart of the dummy and leave the sword stuck in it.

On the third leg, pick up your waiting lance and thread two rings and a peg on the end of it.

From go to whoa you are allowed 50 seconds, or 45 seconds if the jumps are not included.

At this point it is abundantly clear that children do not have all the fun in mounted games! Racing around with a sword or lance and gun, dispatching dowel rods and slicing lemons attracts just the sort of grown-up you think it would: calm, controlled, patient, with good eye/hand coordination and a well-developed sense of humour.

This is because it takes a tremendous amount of practice and self-discipline to perform each of these moves to the point where they are second nature. Hooligans are attracted to this event but they don't last long, any more then they did in the real cavalry. Every single time you pick up a sword or lance it has to be done *right* for your safety and that of your horse and team-mates. There is no such thing as just going through it and getting the feel of it. In every single run, whether it is done at the walk, the trot, the canter or the full gallop, the pressure is on and most of it is on the rider.

Flying lead changes are not important. Bending is not particularly so. But control is everything. The horses must walk out in line like good little school children and they must stop, go and work closely together, side by side if the occasion demands. A tent-pegger must be able to take his horse for granted, and he spends a terrific amount of time looking for and training a horse he can depend on utterly.

A good coach begins by working his class quietly after warming up the horses and riders thoroughly. The team begins working on their weapon drill and weapon handling skills individually with the coach correcting their faults one at time. Then the riders work in pairs, coordinating their actions as a team. Finally they work in fours.

At that point the coach begins studying the horses to see which horse works best in which position. Some horses will want to be out in front, while others feel more secure surrounded by their friends in the middle. Quarter Horses, Australian Stock Horses and cross-breds are particularly good for this sport although Thoroughbreds have been very successful and the Army swore by them. What you want is a horse that will do short sprints of

120–130m (125–135 yards) at the gallop and keep his head. The hard part for any horse is the discipline required to walk in quietly and line up, then peel off one at a time at the gallop, only to halt hard and walk quietly and neatly in formation. Time and time again.

Tent-pegging is a highly coordinated sport and both horse and rider have to be taught. A team is judged on drill as well as on the actual pegging, and winning and losing often hang on the entry and exit of a tent-pegger's horse. You have to know that your horse is going to halt at the required time and place without a lot of conversation about it. You shouldn't have to guide your horse. He must know exactly what to do and, after months and months of practice, he will.

If you keep in mind the principles of training that we have been discussing all along, tent-pegging or any other mounted game will not ruin your horse or pony for other events. (Although there is a little conflict in polo-crosse/polo and tent-pegging because in polo the horse learns to move with you when you shift your weight. In tent-pegging when you move or lean down, the horse must ignore this and continue to run straight.)

Tent-pegging and other mounted games will make you a better rider. Timing and coordination are everything to a tent-pegger but a successful competitor in this sport is also a master of sports psychology. As Colin Campbell, Australian National Tent-pegging Coach says, 'Keep your head with your body. What I mean is, don't worry about things you can't change when you are riding in competition. You may see the peg and think "Oh, it might have a knot in it." Forget that! Control what you can. Don't worry about anything that is beyond your control. Don't put your mind out in front. Concentrate on what you are doing now.

'For example, when you line up for the salute, think about what you are doing then, not what you will be doing later. Think about the salute not, "Oh, look where they have put the umbrella!"'

He is completely right. There is enough to concentrate on. A tent-pegger has no time to worry. Don't watch the lance point, watch the peg. Hit it a couple of inches above ground. The momentum of the horse will carry you past and the lance will fly right back. Let the lance come over your shoulder. Turn your face to watch the block on the end of the lance and count: 1 . . . 2 . . .

and swing the lance back into position. Don't look *under* your arm as this throws your body forward and can cause the horse to stumble.

The more you learn, the more you need to learn. Just like any other mounted game.

13

Competitions in General

At this point, if our horse knows all his basics, we can take him out in company and test him. This is not the culmination of the games horse's training, it is just the beginning of a new stage in his training. We may be entering gymkhanas and rallies but not with an idea of actually competing. As the Australians say, 'We are donating our entry fees.' We are putting our horse in a competition to see what kind of a response we can get from him.

Admittedly in the beginning it seems like the only response we are getting is bad.

Like steeplechasers, flat-racers and Standardbreds, mounted games horses go through several stages of development when they actually begin to compete against other horses. Just look at the old, experienced racehorses. They walk up to the gate looking calm but interested – and then BANG – they're off and running. Young green racehorses are thinking about the noise, the other horses, the people – anything except about what they are there for. These inexperienced horses are excited and unsure of what is going to happen next.

Our games horse may be side-passing through his poles at the canter beautifully at home, he may be the soul of concentration and agility in his own arena. Even so, he is not a made games horse yet . . . not by any means. In his first season he is without competition experience and therefore an unknown quantity.

The common experience of gymkhana horse trainers, whether those trainers are professionals, teenagers or champion novices, is usually the same:

'The horse goes into an unfamiliar arena and he is looking at the other horses and the audience and not concentrating on his cues. I take him down the poles, turn him around and get him weaving back through them. Just as he is nearly finished with the pattern and I am wondering if my horse has learned anything, it suddenly occurs to him "Hey! I'm in the poles!' Now he is responding and concentrating so I turn him loose, race him through the few remaining poles . . . and fail to make up the lost time.'

This is not typical of just the first competition: it applies the whole first season of competition. And you have to keep this in mind and not punish the horse. When he goes into a rally or show arena, you are teaching him something new. It may be based on what he he has already learned at home but it is still a whole new phase of training.

The next season the horse will take one look at the poles or sacks or pegs or whatever and he will know exactly what to do with them. He won't be thinking about the crowds or the loudspeaker. He will think 'Aha! The poles! Time to run. Now I wonder how sloppy I can get and still get the job done?' At this point the horse might start picking up bad habits, like forgetting to keep his hindquarters under him or leaning into the poles. Maybe his attitude is good but he is sore somewhere and we don't know about it. Maybe he is too excited and we must take the time to calm him down.

Maybe we have been pushing him too hard and the horse is panicking under the pressure. So we will back off and take things slower and rebuild his confidence. Remember, a horse can get overfaced by speed just as he can by jumps that are too high or rides that are too long.

But if we keep our head and hold our temper the horse will come to us and everything will begin falling into place. We will begin saying to our friends and family 'This horse is fantastic! This horse will burn them up!' Then something else goes wrong and we have to take the time to correct it.

By the third season the horse is trained and experienced. He walks into the ring with interest and concentration rather than uncertainty. At this point we are letting the horse run and make his little mistakes. We can compensate for them with our body and timing. Each time we go into the arena we try to do well in terms of balance and position. We don't want to scare the horse or overface him. We want him to like his work, not fear it. If this means sacrificing a few seconds to position him or hold him back to keep his balance, we do it. The ribbon is not the important thing. Our horse is learning his trade and this is his on-the-job training, nothing more.

Only when he is ready to compete safely do we start asking him for serious competition. At this point we are not entering the class for experience. We are entering to win.

At this point we can demand more. We begin riding him twice a day if we are getting ready for a big competition. His daily training has built his muscles, timing and wind so we can stress him without hurting him. Now we want our horse responding immediately to our legs. Not two beats later, but now! We dig with our heels going around the end pole to get him down and digging with his hind legs.

This doesn't mean we are running our games horse every day, or even that we do a complete pattern every day. So many people have an unclear idea of how a games horse should be exercised. These people come home from work or from school, saddle their pony and ride him for ten minutes, racing through pattern after pattern, whipping and spurring. They then cool down the pony and put him away. Every day this animal is introduced to running flat out, never to stop. A week or two of this and he quickly becomes a raving idiot. Quiet, steady work, like cross-country trotting, is what these horses and ponies need to keep them physically and mentally fit.

If you must do any pattern work at all with an experienced horse then just trot him five or six times through the pattern and then do something completely different, leaving that day's practice on his mind. Or do a pattern at a fast trot, taking hold of the horse and moving him over hard and fast going through the poles, for instance. A word of advice here: don't do these exercises at a canter. An extended trot is just as good for him and it is easier to balance a horse at the trot.

After we have done these gymnastic exercises once or twice at the trot, we might let another rider canter him easily round the paddock or turn him out to graze or we could take him cross-country. This cross-country work isn't just good for his mental outlook; it also makes a games horse faster. A games horse, like any other sprinter, needs a lot of wind and the best way to develop it is by trotting him long distances or up gradual inclines.

That is the sensible approach. But it is very hard for a games rider not to run a pattern or two every day just to see if the speed is still there. You have to trust your training. Leave his mind alone and work on his body instead. Take him out of the arena and let him do extended trot through the woods.

This kind of work calms the horse down and dispels the notion that every time a saddle is put on him, he has to deliver speed. Once your horse knows the patterns and the cues to perform them, he should rarely see those poles or patterns outside the show ring. It is possible to compete every week and ride during the week but riding does not mean riding the pattern. Take the horse trail riding, work on his problems at the trot, or just ride him in the arena. Once your horse is trained keep him in condition like any other performance horse: walk, trot, canter, perhaps go hunting. You may run your horse through the patterns once during the week to keep him sharp, but once would be enough.

14

Competing

Upon arriving at the show and unpacking everything, the best way to warm up a mounted games horse is the same way we warm up a dressage horse, show jumper or hack. In the working-in arena just follow his usual routine of walk, trot, canter and review. Let him look at things and get the lie of the land. In the early days of competing with a green horse or pony, walk him around a pole or rubbish bin just so that he will get an idea of what he will see in the arena. Consider circling the barrel at a walk or slowly side-passing through a pole in the same way a show jumper is shown his practice jump.

The next thing to do is study the arena or the area where the games will be run. If the ground is sticky or hard and slippery, back off – not just for your own sake but also for the safety of your horse. This does not mean you scratch the class, just that you do not run flat out and you do not take chances. Studs or borium do not guarantee that the horse will not slip on a very hard or very soft surface. They merely help him avoid slipping. No ribbon nor any amount of points is worth risking your life or limbs or those of your horse.

All things being equal, however, try to move off the starting line with some speed, keeping in mind that with a young horse it will take a lot of control to make his first turn or halt. The faster you go at the start, the less likely you are to be able to produce that control. It will be even harder if the horse is distracted by his surroundings. Therefore, in the beginning of his season or career, don't worry about winning the class. Worry about keeping the horse relaxed, balanced and comfortable. This means not leaving the starting line any faster than the horse can easily handle.

There is a temptation to want to win immediately and many people give in to that temptation. By creating speed and pressure that neither they nor their horse can handle, they quickly turn their horse into a bundle of frayed nerves and he soon has to be dragged rearing and bucking into the ring. Even if they win their first class or heat, these riders will have pushed their horse beyond his capacity. Controlling the horse at speeds he cannot handle becomes a problem. The rider thinks that the only way to solve it is with a stronger bit. 'Let's put a bit in his mouth with a port that reaches to his eyeballs and then run barbed wire through his nostrils and *that* will teach him to turn and stop.

It is much better to be sensible and deal in the realms of the possible. When entering these early classes, just sit back and smile and concentrate on teaching your horse. Keep him steady now and when he can handle his speed he will be very competitive.

The best thing gymkhana horses and ponies can do is walk around between heats or classes. Think about having a friend (an experienced rider) sit on your horse between classes. Let him walk the horse around, give him a drink and let him calm down and forget the excitement of running. The horse that has to be lead into the ring is the one which has not been taught how to let down and relax between runs. The consistent winner is the one who gets his horse walked out and sensible again before he puts him up or takes him out again. This cooling down isn't just good for the horse mentally, although it does encourage him to be calm. Walking around, having a few sips of water and generally unwinding also give him a chance to catch his breath for the next heat. His pulse and respiration can return to normal and he will have that much more to run with in the next round.

The horse's mind isn't the only one to work in competitive mounted games. Psychology of the rider and his competition plays a big part too. As soon as you break a rider's concentration, you are on your way to beating him. Here is how one prominent games rider uses gamesmanship on himself and the competition:

'I try to talk to all the people I am riding against. I get a feeling of them and their personalities. I might say, "You're going to have to take it easy on me. I'm getting old and you've got a nice horse, so just take it easy on the old guy." They just laugh but they are thinking about me now and not how they are going to ride the class.

'If I was just starting out, if I didn't have a reputation, I'd try to get the competition thinking in general, play on their nerves and sensitivity. Once they start second guessing themselves and changing their strategy, they have lost their concentration. Anything I can do, I will do to get their mind off their business and onto mine.

'I don't think about the competition as such. I'm thinking of my strategy, how to beat them and I'm psyching myself up. I watch the other horses run. I find out everything I can before I go in the arena: where the slippery spots are, where there might be a distraction. . .

'Another thing is to get aggressive without getting angry or made. I just mutter, "OK, I've had it. I'm ready. The horse is ready. Now go in there and do it right!" But I do it in cold blood. I don't race into the arena thinking, "Arrh, I'm here! **I'm here!**" Every second of the race I control the horse. I put him where I want him instead of throwing the reins at him and letting him run off in all directions. The horse is within my hands and I am concentrating on the pattern and shaving every single second off it while keeping the horse in balance. If I have broken the other rider's concentration so that he is looking at me instead of thinking about what he is doing, then I am that much more ahead.'

Looking at the other riders is fatal. It is as useless as looking back over a jump to see if the rail has fallen. What are you going to do? Put it back? By twisting to look at the other horses the rider is physically off balance and by letting his attention wander he is mentally unfocused.

Of all the people you ride against, the hot-heads with the whips are the easiest to beat. Instead of positioning their horse, all they have on their mind is blind, uncontrolled speed. These riders push their horses beyond their limits and throw them off balance and into trouble. All you have to do is be smart enough to wait until it happens. The whip-swingers may beat you one time, but you will beat them nine times. They are erratic under any circumstances but when it comes to real pressure where there are prize money or championship points involved, they will fall apart.

Whipping interrupts your horse's concentration and it interrupts the rider's as well. Pretty soon the horse is thinking more about being whipped than he is about running and changing leads. At that point he begins to slow down. Or he begins to dodge to get away from the whip. Or he begins kicking out at it, which throws him more off stride, off balance and slows him down.

And all the time this is happening the rider is whipping the daylights out of the horse, not looking where he is going and all the time hoping that lightening will strike this horse and give him more ability than he has.

It never does.

15

The Set-backs

In spite of the high speeds and intricate gymnastics, a mounted games horse doesn't suffer a higher percentage of physical unsoundnesses than do other performance horses. His problems are the same as those of any other competition-oriented athlete: mental strain and boredom. Long-distance riders, event riders, racehorse riders all face the problem of peaking their horse, bringing him to his physical and mental best at just the right time. It is very hard for the amateur, and especially the professional, to know when he has peaked his horse, when he is at the top of his form (and not getting sick of the whole idea).

In the beginning we take our horse to competitions for the experience. Once he knows his trade we go to earn points in order to qualify for World Championships or Prince Philip Cup or what have you. And when we have reached our goal, then we let our horse rest. We ride him but do no more competitions until the big one we are after.

But most amateur riders don't want to follow that programme. Most riders want to take their horse to shows or rallies every weekend during the season. That's fine and that's the way it should be. But these riders must realise that like any other well-tuned athlete, they and their horses will reach a peak of performance and when they do, they will start a downhill slide. They will start the year pretty well and the horse begins to win. But after a while the horse is not running so fast, or maybe the pony is not going to the gate as well. Maybe he is not eating when he is away from home, or perhaps he is hitting the poles. It could be many things but mostly it is just a dull feeling. He doesn't seem to be the same horse he was when you started the season.

There may be something physically wrong. Do not discount that possibility. Have your horse checked by a veterinarian, a farrier, a horse dentist.

But there is also the possibility that the horse has reached his peak and is tapering off. Many people hit a dry spell and think they'll bring the horse out of it by changing their training methods, changing the horse's personality, maybe using a whip on him during practice. If you try to *work* him out of this tapering off, you will confuse and alienate the horse and disorganise his training programme, and you will not have much of a horse left at the end of the process.

What has happened is that the horse has become tired of this event and he needs some time off or something completely different to do with his time. Many serious amateur riders truly believe that their horse should be in hard athletic training 365 days a year. They think that anything less is not getting sufficient use out of him. But if you suggested that these riders run or work out every day or even six days a week, those riders would be appalled.

Always remember that every athlete, whether he is human or equine, needs a holiday.

If you remember this, you will be able to deal with this downhill slide before it turns into sourness. You will have a successful season and a successful career if you give your horse a break along the way instead of trying to keep him at the top of his form indefinitely. If you keep in mind that horses get tired, you will be able to face the idea that maybe your horse cannot win this event but maybe he can in a month from now when he has had a holiday.

Glossary

Whilst you may think that Canada, America, Australia, New Zealand and all points in between share a common language with the United Kingdom, when you try to write a book on mounted games you realise how wrong you are. There are some readers who may feel that anyone who doesn't know what a halter is really shouldn't be training a horse for mounted games. Rest assured that he probably does know what it is, he just calls it by a different name. In an attempt to head off any misunderstandings, I have included the following notes. Other, less-familiar terms are explained within the text.

BACK UP/REIN BACK: Travel backwards while sitting on a horse.

BOSAL: Bosal is to hackamore what bit is to bridle. A bosal is the stiff ring of rawhide, fibreglass or whatever that goes around the horse's nose and works on the bridge of his nose instead of on the bars of his mouth.

CROSS-BRED: The product of one registered horse and another registered horse not of the same breed, e.g. Arab/Quarter Horse, etc.

CUTTING HORSE: A horse of any breed who participates in cutting. Cutting cattle is separating one beast (cow, steer) from a group of his fellows and making sure he stays separated from them for a given amount of time.

GRADE: Unregistered horse or pony.

HALTER/HEADCOLLAR: There are technical differences but both terms are used interchangeably. It is what you put on a horse's head to lead him or tie him up as opposed to when riding him.

PAINT: An American-origin colour breed now found all over the world.

PALOUSE: An Australian breed of pony with Appaloosa markings. The North American version of this breed is called Pony of the Americas.

PATTERN: Just what it says. The pattern you follow in a game: a cloverleaf pattern for a barrel race; an in-and-out pattern for pole-bending. A 'pattern horse' is one who knows his pattern so well that he really doesn't need much guidance from his rider. A show jumper would use the word 'course' to describe the path he follows; games riders use the word 'pattern'.

QUARTER HORSE: Originally an American breed of stock horse now popular all over the world. Fast, handy and for the most part sensible.

ROMAL: In Western riding there are two types of reins, split and joined. The joined reins are joined on the ends, plaited and sometimes decorated. This join is called a romal.

SIDE-PASS: Moving sideways while seated on a horse.

STANDARDBRED: Horses bred for harness racing (mainly); trotters and pacers.

STOCK HORSE: An Australian Stock Horse is a specific breed but the general term 'stock horse' includes a type of horse used to work stock, i.e. sheep or cattle.

TRAIL RIDING: Going for a ride outside an arena or manège without the benefit of hounds.

TWO-TRACKS: Instead of moving absolutely sideways, the horse moves forward and sideways. (This definition varies from sport to sport and in dressage it would have a more exact definition. However, in this book, two-track and leg yield are two ways of saying the same thing.)

Useful Addresses

Canada
Canadian Equestrian Federation
1600 James Naismith Dr.
Gloucester
Ontario K1B 5N4

Canadian Pony Club
11B Laidlaw Blvd
Markham
Ontario L3P 1W5

Canadian Quarter Horse Association
D St.
PO Box 6950
Calgary
Alberta

United Kingdom
Mounted Games Association of Great Britain
Bunces Farm
Runwick
Farnham
Surrey

British Horse Society
British Equestrian Centre
Stoneleigh Park
Kenilworth
Warwickshire, CV8 2LR

Pony Club
c/o British Horse Society (see above)

The Western Horsemens Association of Great Britain
13 East View
Barnet
Hertfordshire
EN5 5TL

Australia
Equestrian Federation of Australia
GPO Box 4317
Sydney, NSW 2001

Australian Pony Club Council
PO Box 46
Lockhart, NSW 2656

Australian Quarter Horse Association
PO Box 979
Tamworth, NSW 2340

Australian Tentpegging Association
Sec. Allan Bradshaw
93 Hardinge St.
Deniliquin, NSW 2710

Australian Pro-Rodeo Association
Sec. Peter Cook
Box 264, Warwick 4370

United States
United States Pony Club
303 High Street
West Chester, PA 19380

American Horse Show Association
598 Madison Avenue
New York, NY 10022

American Horse Council
1700 K St. NW
Washington DC 20006

4H Clubs can be contacted through the State College
of Agriculture in individual states.

Pony of the Americas Association
Mason City, Iowa 50401

Women's Professional Rodeo Association
Rte 5 Box 698
Blanchard, Oklahoma 73010

American Quarter Horse Association
PO Box 32470
Amarillo, Texas 79120

New Zealand
New Zealand Horse Society
PO Box 47
Hastings, N.I.

Pony Club Association
Sec. Mrs Judy Wakeling
Katitieke
RD 2
Owhango, N.I.

South Africa
South African National Equestrian Federation
PO Box 69414
Bryanston 2021